CAPTURING FINANCE

Capturing Finance · ARBITRAGE AND SOCIAL DOMINATION

Carolyn Hardin

DUKE UNIVERSITY PRESS *Durham and London* 2021

Designed by Matthew Tauch
Typeset in Arno Pro Regular by Westchester Publishing
Services

Library of Congress Cataloging-in-Publication Data
Names: Hardin, Carolyn F., [date] author.
Title: Capturing finance : arbitrage and social domination /
Carolyn Hardin.
Description: Durham : Duke University Press, 2021. | Includes
bibliographical references and index.
Identifiers: LCCN 2020042609 (print) | LCCN 2020042610 (ebook)
ISBN 9781478013389 (hardcover)
ISBN 9781478014294 (paperback)
ISBN 9781478021605 (ebook)
Subjects: LCSH: Arbitrage. | Risk. | Finance. | Capitalism.
Classification: LCC HG6024.A3 H367 2021 (print) | LCC HG6024.A3
(ebook) | DDC 332.64/5—dc23
LC record available at https://lccn.loc.gov/2020042609
LC ebook record available at https://lccn.loc.gov/2020042610

Cover art: Justine Smith, *A Bigger Bang*, 2009. Bank notes on
paper, 137.5 × 101.5 cm. Courtesy of the artist.

This book is dedicated to Ted,
my anchor in this world.

CONTENTS

ACKNOWLEDGMENTS

The inspiration for this book came from my time at Kenan-Flagler Business School, during which I was mystified to hear the word *arbitrage* reverberating in every classroom. I was privileged to have excellent professors and mentors there who taught me financial economics and supported my research, including Alexander Arapoglou, Diego Garcia, Günter Strobl, and Ed Van Wesep.

Between the years 2013 and 2016, I participated in a number of institutes, seminars, symposia, and workshops with the Cultures of Finance Working Group at New York University. My relatively late entry into this incredible network of scholars meant that I was just beginning to form the ideas communicated in this book when they were coming in for a landing with their collective work. The result, *Derivatives and the Wealth of Societies*, features less in this book than it perhaps should, as its chapters represent the final crystallizations of projects I got to hear about in several stages over the course of those years. All of which is to say, the work of Arjun Appadurai, Elie Ayache, Emanuel Derman, Benjamin Lee, Edward LiPuma, Randy Martin, Robert Meister, and especially Robert Wosnitzer fashions a bedrock upon which this book sits. Their friendship was no less helpful to the project, especially Robert Wosnitzer's. His willingness to talk me through the intricacies of capital markets and securitization over and over was nothing short of saintly. Robert is a dedicated confidant and supporter whose generosity I have tried and failed to emulate. I am a better scholar and person for knowing him.

I was inspired by Dick Bryan and Michael Rafferty's innovative work in political economy and finance before I met either of them. Dick was a member of my dissertation committee who molded and directed this work. He also used his position and influence to, both figuratively and literally, give me a seat at the table. I am indebted to him for his firm but gentle instruction, mentorship, friendship, and generosity.

Nothing I could write here would quantify Larry Grossberg's influence on my ways of thinking or scholarship. He directed the original project upon which this book is based, encouraged me to think and work outside the box, shepherded me when I got lost, and gave me the space, time, and resources to do weird and surprising work. Best of all, he taught me to *think* cultural studies, a skill that has paid incredible dividends. He has all my gratitude.

Editorial review isn't always edifying. In this case, it very much was. Courtney Berger provided the perfect combination of encouragement and advice, which helped me write a better book. The referees who read and commented on this manuscript were far gentler and more constructive than they had to be. Their insightful suggestions coaxed connections out of the work that now look obvious, but which I could not see by myself. I am grateful for their invaluable assistance in improving the book.

There is a business of Mongeese at Miami University in Ohio that fashions the kind of support network you would expect from fearsome predators who are also adorable and fun. Matt Crain, Katie Day Good, Mack Hagood, Hongmei Li, Andrew Peck, Rosemary Pennington, Andy Rice, Adam Rottinghaus, and John Tchernev are the best group of early-career colleagues a scholar could hope for. I'm grateful to them for the celebrations and commiserations that made this process more bearable.

I must also thank a number of people who were supportive, helpful, and generous in various ways during the writing of this book: Fiona Allon, Ivan Ascher, Ron Becker, Melinda Cooper, Martijn Konings, Chris Lundberg, Michael Palm, Michael Pryke, Sarah Sharma, and Armond Towns. Thanks to Adam Rottinghaus and Corey Riggenbach for their illustrations. Thanks to Luke Imes for his assistance in formatting the manuscript. Thank you to my mother, Mary Richter, for her keen editorial eye, encouragement, and numerous suggestions and conversations. Thank you to J Nikol Jackson-Beckham for giving me the kind of day-to-day support that can only come from a best friend. Finally, my greatest appreciation goes to my family for supporting and distracting me in the most helpful ways.

Into the Lions' Den

In the fall of 2007, I entered graduate school to pursue my master's degree in communication studies during the same month as the so-called credit crunch—the seizing up of bank-to-bank lending amid uncertainty about the value of mortgage-backed securities. This, it would turn out, was the first act of the global financial crisis, and my postsecondary work quickly turned to issues economic. By the fall 2009, when I began my PhD studies, I was working with professors and graduate student colleagues to try to make sense of the unfolding crisis. As an interdisciplinary scholar, I felt it was important to put my money where my mouth is (or my mouth where the money is in this case) and take some actual finance courses. With an undergraduate degree in mathematics, I felt confident I could do the work. So, in the fall of 2010, after taking two semesters of prerequisites in the economics department and with the support of my advisor, I enrolled in "Introduction to Derivatives," in the Master of Business Administration program at the business school at my university.

After three years of reading critiques of capitalism and the crisis, I approached the gilded complex of marble staircases and soaring arches located far away from the shabbier digs of the humanities departments with trepidation. I was going into the lions' den; the home of the "masters of the universe" (Wolfe 1988) who had inflicted a recession on the world. I naively believed that since I was a critical researcher, we were naturally at odds. I expected to be met with suspicion and antipathy, and steeled myself for the interactions to come.

My actual experience at the business school surprised me in two distinct ways that would turn out to be intimately related. First, I was welcomed with warmth and interest into the very belly of the beast.[1] And, second, the topics covered in my MBA classes were virtually all overrun by one particular term, *arbitrage*. As I would discover, arbitrage is a label applied to a particular sort of trade wherein the trader borrows money to buy a cheap security in one market and then sells the same or similar security for a higher price elsewhere, netting a profit. But this was as yet unexplained. All I knew was that my derivatives professor used the term frequently and blithely, as if it was as banal and fundamental as oxygen itself, and I had never so much as read the term.

I have come to believe that the first surprise—my good treatment by my finance professors and classmates—reflects the failure of critical scholars to truly grasp or challenge the very real problems with finance as it is taught and practiced. If we did, finance professors might well regard us with caution. That we don't was perfectly crystallized in my experience from day one of hearing over and over again about arbitrage, a concept that not one of capitalism's critics (that I had yet encountered) had even alluded to, much less unpacked. Arbitrage was clearly fundamental to academic finance, and I didn't even know what it is. It is possible that arbitrage would not have borne down on my thinking so substantially if I had found myself in "Corporate Finance" or "Microeconomics" in my first term at the business school. But since derivatives played such a large role in the financial crisis, it seemed a fitting place to start. And, even after completing that course, I found arbitrage at least mentioned in all my other classes. It was always present, never questioned, never critiqued. It was the substrate of financial economics, and I wanted to know why.

In the textbooks I was using, arbitrage was always at least defined, though those definitions differed across sources. In some definitions, like this one, "Arbitrage is the process of buying assets in one market and selling them in another to profit from unjustifiable price differences," arbitrage is restricted to the act of buying a set of securities and selling that same set again (Billingsley 2006, 2). In others, like this one, "a trading strategy that takes advantage of two or more securities being mispriced relative to each other," it may be securities that are equivalent though not truly the same (Hull 2008, 521). The key to the definition is that this buying and selling takes place because there are different prices in different markets in which the securities are bought and sold. In the act of buying the low-priced security and selling the high-priced security, a profit is gained.

All definitions of arbitrage include two caveats, which turn out to be of key importance to its role in financial economics. First, to be arbitrage, the trade must always be "self-financing," that is, done with borrowed money and not the trader's own capital (Billingsley 2006, 2). Second, many definitions include the restriction that trading be done simultaneously or instantaneously. These conditions differentiate arbitrage from risky investing in stocks or practices of transporting goods (merchanting). Unlike the stock speculator or merchant who has skin in the game by way of his investment and/or his possession of assets over time, the arbitrageur must make a profit without using his own money or risking that his goods are destroyed or his stock depreciates. Arbitrage is only arbitrage if it is *riskless*.[2]

The assertion that arbitrage is riskless isn't a mere rhetorical flourish. It is the reason for arbitrage's centrality in all my finance classes. Arbitrage is the exception that proves the rule that all returns above some baseline— the risk-free return—are based on some kind of risk. Financial economics operates on the basic principle that risk and return are directly correlated; as one goes up, so must the other. There is no such thing as a free lunch or money for nothing. You must take the chance that the company you are investing in might falter or fail altogether, or that the yields of a commodity will be down compared to expectations. The magnitude of the risk you take on corresponds to the returns you can expect if things go well, at least in theory. In theory, securities do not offer high returns for low risk. If they did, investors would flock to them, diluting returns. This works in the converse case of low return and high risk. The basic concepts of supply and demand thus ensure that risk and return are properly balanced, or so the logic goes.

The relationship between risk and return underscores every part of the imaginary universe of efficient markets that financial economics describes. In this universe, riskless profit is an oxymoron. Profit or return is the correlate of risk. Without one, you cannot have the other. Therefore, in the theoretical world of finance, arbitrage is actually impossible. Of course, this prompts the question: If it is impossible, why is it so central to financial theory? It turns out that arbitrage occupies a privileged and bizarre ontological position in the world of finance. In financial economics, it is enshrined in the "no-arbitrage condition," which is used to construct modern financial pricing models. The reason I heard the word *arbitrage* so much in "Introduction to Derivatives" is that derivatives pricing is deduced from a theoretical trading situation in which arbitrage *cannot* occur. A call option—a financial contract that gives the buyer the option to purchase stock at a future date—is priced correctly if the price does *not* allow a trader to arbitrage between the option and its underlying stock. If arbitrage is possible, the price is wrong and the seller is allowing the buyer to gain riskless profit, a challenge to the very foundation on which finance is built. For financial theory, then, arbitrage is present only in its absence, that is, in the "no-arbitrage condition" (Bodie, Kane, and Marcus 2009, 325).

Of course, the world does not function exactly as financial economic theorems and models dictate, but that does not mean that the strange presence-in-absence of arbitrage doesn't matter. When discussing actually existing markets—the kind that can be inefficient, and where market prices can get, if only momentarily, out of whack—economists reference arbitrage not as an impossibility, for it does in fact occur, but as an automatic mechanism that will return prices to correct levels through the fundamental logic of supply and demand. That is, if prices for the same asset occur at different levels in different markets, arbitrageurs will spring into action, buying the cheap and selling the dear, thus increasing demand (and price) for the first and increasing supply (and thereby lowering price) for the second. Arbitrage, despite its absence being the very condition of financial models, becomes the proof that if they are ever violated in practice, it won't be for long. Arbitrage is assumed to be both absent as a condition of formal economic models, and present as the assumed real-world mechanism that polices the system to bring it in line with the models. In this second role, arbitrage occupies a privileged position not only in financial economics, but in the broader neoliberal vision of the market as a more perfect information processor than any human brain could hope to be. Arbitrage is framed as the logical guarantor of market efficiency, a moral imperative, and a public good, which imposes fairness in financial markets. Regulators specifically point to "arbitrage discipline" as the reason that regulations are not needed in financial markets (Roye 2001)!

Yet financial traders are not interested in performing arbitrage out of an altruistic desire to create efficient markets. They are interested in profit, and that interest is what makes arbitrage the efficiency-enforcing practice that it is (some of the time). What's more, as long as arbitrage is considered riskless and therefore immediately bookable, it has immediate and attractive material benefits to traders who receive bonuses based on their booked profit. Other strategies that involve seeking profit that might or might not materialize (long-term investing, venture capital, etc.) pale in comparison. In this way, in the world of finance, arbitrage is something of a golden goose, or, to use language more familiar to the world of finance, it's the proverbial free lunch. Arbitrage is money for nothing, return without having to pay the piper for risk. The profit made from arbitrage is sought by traders *because* it violates the very laws of finance that it supposedly promotes, that is, because it is, at least in theory, *riskless*, secure, and therefore immediately bookable as profit in traders' accounts.

In this system of thought, everyone wins because "making markets efficient can be a profitable activity" (O'Hara 2016, 27). Yet the fact that arbitrage may, as a seeming side effect of its true goal, provide a profit to those who undertake it is nowhere systematically assessed in financial economics. For all the attention given to the system-wide benefit of arbitrage—market efficiency—no assessment of the systemic impacts of arbitrage profit is offered. This is a serious omission given the evidence that arbitrage has been the main focus of financial traders for at least a century. An 1892 article in the *New York Times* declared, "It is alleged that probably three-fourths of all the business done at the Exchange is transacted through arbitrage houses."[3] An American Management Association newsletter written in 1984—as computerized trading was allowing new forms of arbitrage—claimed that the "emphasis on arbitrage . . . is already well on its way to revolutionizing corporate attitudes and practices" (Militello 1984, 29). Similarly, in 1986 Richard Croft reported that "some analysts think that as much as 40 per cent of all trading on the New York Stock Exchange is, in fact, [index] arbitrage" and that the "number and range of participants continue to grow."[4] A 2003 article in *Financial Times* quoted hedge fund manager Andy Preston as saying that "over the past five years [arbitrage] strategies have become increasingly sought after because they have delivered phenomenal returns."[5] In 2014 Mark Blyth, a professor of political economy at Brown University, quoted a statistic eerily similar to the one offered in the *New York Times* in 1892: "A funny thing about these very big banks . . . they make 70 percent of their profits through trading, basically swapping bits of paper with each other for arbitrage gains, none of which arguably adds to anything except global liquidity and doesn't really do much for real investment" ("Credit Suisse" 2014). Finally, in 2016 finance professor Maureen O'Hara declared that "arbitrage is a ubiquitous activity in financial markets" (26). What's more, as I demonstrate, an arbitrage trade in large part inflated the housing bubble. The production of all those financial derivatives, mortgage-backed securities, collateralized debt obligations, credit default swaps, and more, was directed toward an arbitrage trade of epic proportions.

....

After discovering arbitrage, I set about constructing my own reading list of noneconomists who have written about it. That list is populated almost entirely by economic sociologists in the subfield termed social studies of finance (SSF) and anthropologists, who, in the early to mid-2000s, began to pay special attention to arbitrage (Beunza, Hardie, and MacKenzie 2006; Beunza and Stark 2004; Hardie 2004; MacKenzie 2003; Miyazaki 2007; Zaloom 2006). These researchers attempted to call collective attention to the fact that arbitrage had become a "form of trading crucial both to the modern theory of finance and to market practice" (Beunza, Hardie, and MacKenzie 2006, 721). Donald MacKenzie's widely read *An Engine Not a Camera* explained the way that arbitrage functioned to bring markets in line with the models practitioners used—something he termed, following the work of Michel Callon, "performativity." However, in accordance with much of SSF, these investigations did not submit arbitrage to critical scrutiny by, for example, radically deconstructing the financial economic definition of the term. Instead, they focused on the material and social aspects of arbitrage in practice. Indeed, Beunza, Hardie, and MacKenzie hoped that "the study of arbitrage could be a productive area of collaboration [with] financial economics" (2006, 741).

Anthropologist Hirokazu Miyazaki contributed articles and a full-length book on his study of arbitrageurs in Japan. Like the sociologists, he also notes that arbitrage is "a central category of financial economics and a widely deployed trading strategy" (2013, 8). His study gives important indications of just how central arbitrage is when he claims that, "for the arbitrageurs I knew, arbitrage was both their individual action and the market mechanism itself" (21). Miyazaki (2007) pushes past the SSF capitulation to financial economics by questioning the strict distinction between speculation and arbitrage. However, rather than examining the broad political and economic effects of arbitrage trading, his study focuses on reframing financial market professionals as philosophers whose entire orientation to reality takes on the qualities of arbitrage. For Miyazaki, arbitrage is a metaphor for the "daily comparative work of Japanese financial professionals" in seeking arbitrage opportunities and also defining their own identities and personal goals (2013, 13).

While these contributions brought attention to the practice of arbitrage, they failed to rise to the level of critique, as they did not question whether it is really the neutral trading strategy it is argued to be. Nor did they question the politics of—the relations of power produced, reified, and required for—this most central of financial concepts and practices. I have found two exceptions. The first is the edited volume *Derivatives and the Wealth of Societies*, written by a group of scholars who pay close attention to arbitrage and its role in the social and cultural constitution of markets (Lee and Martin 2016). I had the benefit of attending many events with the working group that produced the book, and it influenced my thinking in several ways. Second, in 2016 finance professor Maureen O'Hara published *Something for Nothing: Arbitrage and Ethics on Wall Street*, in which she set herself the task of "trying to put ethics and finance together" (viii), a laudable endeavor, especially when she explains that "what is unethical is not readily apparent to a surprising number of people on Wall Street and on Main Street" (3). However, it quickly becomes apparent that, while O'Hara believes that arbitrage may sometimes be "used to exploit others, [and] to take advantage of the complexity in modern markets to behave unethically," she does not question the definition of arbitrage as that which promotes efficiency within markets (3). Instead, she reiterates that, "regardless of the setting, arbitrage also makes markets better because, with prices aligned, resources can be allocated to their most efficient uses" (27). She even explains that the "something for nothing" title of her book refers not to the riskless profit that arbitrageurs enjoy, but to the "tremendous benefits to the economy, allowing resources to go to their best uses at essentially little or no cost" that arbitrage provides (2), a clear endorsement of arbitrage's efficiency-promoting function, or what I will call the *benevolent-efficiency narrative*.

Something for Nothing turns out to be a careful and well-reasoned attempt to interrogate the ethics of arbitrage from inside the model world in which it is already assumed to be a public good. But this is an impossible effort. O'Hara's focus on the common good is antithetical to the very logic of arbitrage, which I will show is the form of monopolistic appropriation or capture that makes financial capitalism what it is. She is therefore left cataloging various forms of arbitrage along a spectrum from "weasel" to "felon" (2016, 64). For example, she recounts the arbitrage that JP Morgan Chase undertook in California energy markets. Using the price quoting structure of the California Independent System Operator (CAISO), which aggregates bids by energy suppliers, JP Morgan Chase found a way to profit through complex arbitrage schemes that involved placing and removing bids. According to the Federal Energy Regulatory Commission, the trades cost CAISO \$124 million in a little over a year, a shortfall almost certainly passed on to consumers (115).

Yet, from within the benevolent-efficiency narrative, O'Hara wrestles with the ethics of the case. She says that "there will always be winners and losers . . . being a winner is not a crime" (115), but ultimately does label this case as unethical because JP Morgan Chase "ignored the larger ramifications of these actions on everyone else" (117). Her diagnosis contradicts the logic of arbitrage pricing enshrined in the heart of financial economics, and the grander logic of free market capitalism. Arbitrageurs—like the self-interested protagonists animating Adam Smith's invisible hand—are specifically not supposed to consider others. One popular textbook explains: "The idea that market prices will move to rule out arbitrage opportunities is perhaps the most fundamental concept in capital market theory. Violation of this restriction would indicate the grossest form of market irrationality. The critical property of [arbitrage] is that any investor, regardless of risk aversion or wealth, will want to take an *infinite* position in it" (Bodie, Kane, and Marcus 325; my emphasis). Arbitrageurs' pure self-interest is what ensures efficient markets. So O'Hara's suggestion that self-interested motivation in trading is unethical means that—in her framework—all arbitrage is as well.

The ethics of individual arbitrage trading is not the subject of this study. But I do offer an interpretation of arbitrage that can explain O'Hara's contradictory attempt to parse its ethics. My assertion is that arbitrage is central to finance, that it is in fact what makes finance distinct, and that as such it is well overdue for critical scrutiny. In the course of deconstructing the financial economic definition of arbitrage, offering one of my own, and exploring the social conditions that enable it, I take up political rather than ethical questions. I show how arbitrage drove the housing bubble that led to the financial crisis. I also explore the ways that the concept of risk—and particularly of the notions that risk is an objective, measurable characteristic of securities and that risk and return are naturally correlated—created historical social relations that made arbitrage possible and justifiable. And I sketch some preliminary thoughts on how a politics directed at risk might lead to more successful challenges to the worst consequences of financial capitalism.

The book unfolds in two parts corresponding to arbitrage itself on the one hand, and the role of risk in promoting and justifying arbitrage on the other. In chapter 1, I propose a framework for understanding capitalism as an internally differentiated system comprising various apparatuses of capture. Drawing on the work of Moishe Postone (1993), I argue that each form of capture is organized around a particular principle of "abstract domination" that presents itself as quasi-objective and thereby compels the participation of people in the very practice that dominates their lives (Postone 1993, 161, 5). I explore three apparatuses, the industrial capitalism explained by Karl Marx, the racial capitalism that runs from the origins of racial slavery through the present, and financial capitalism. I put this framework in conversation with traditional Marxist understandings of finance and suggest that previous challenges to finance such as Occupy Wall Street have largely failed because they have not focused attention on the principle around which the abstract domination of finance is organized—risk.

In chapter 2, I take on the mainstream financial economic definition of arbitrage. I argue that financial economics and its benevolent-efficiency narrative of arbitrage actually function as a justifying discourse for financial capture that has influenced economic policy, financial regulation, and law. The theoretical role that arbitrage plays in financial economics provides an effective justification and defense of financial capture. However, financial economics doesn't attend to the impacts of arbitrage and the profits it generates in real life. Therefore, it is necessary to construct a new definition based on the functioning of arbitrage in actual financial markets.

This is precisely the task I take up in chapter 3. Through a series of historical case studies, I show that real-life arbitrage is best defined as those kinds of financial trading in which buying and selling instantaneously is *simulated*. Instantaneity is simulated through the use of financial contracts— which stabilize prices over time—or what I call network differentials, differences in connectivity or speed that give some traders advantages over others. In real life, arbitrage is not a benevolent service provided by rational traders, but a battle for simulated instantaneity, fought with ever more complicated derivatives contracts and ever faster and more proprietary network technologies.

The second part of the book turns to the idea of risk as the principle that organizes the system of finance. In chapter 4, I more fully develop the notion of abstract domination by taking a detour through Postone's critique of Marxism. I show that, while exploitation may seem like a reasonable way to interpret arbitrage, it is better to see it as the result of a new system of abstract domination that we have yet to come to terms with. In this system, individuals are compelled to engage in financial risk-taking, and to submit themselves as credit risks in order to borrow money. These activities, risky investing and risky borrowing, produce flows of financial securities that serve as the fertile ground for arbitrage in financial markets.

In chapter 5, I identify the form of arbitrage I call *money machines*. These trades are exceptional in both the sense of being the exception to dominant definitions of arbitrage and of being the most effective, profit-generating way to perform arbitrage. In general, money machine arbitrage trades do not result in prices converging toward equilibrium but instead deliver continuous profits. They therefore thoroughly contradict the benevolent-efficiency narrative that arbitrage makes market prices fair and is self-negating. I show that arbitrage in subprime mortgage–backed securities, particularly those known as collateralized debt obligations (CDOS), in the run-up to the financial crisis was a money machine trade. I conclude this chapter by detailing the structural conditions that allowed financial firms to perform "alchemy" (Benmelech and Dlugosz 2009) on mortgage-backed securities so as to continuously generate profit.

In chapter 6, I reexamine the causes of the financial crisis through the capture framework as a way to account for the systematic nature of financial capitalism and its devastating consequences. I explain the way that both financial credit rating agencies and subprime lending contributed to the crisis by showing how the axiom of risk and return and the axiom of risk measurement shaped each practice. I demonstrate that, contra the accepted wisdom, the risk of subprime CDOS was not inaccurately measured in the run-up to the financial crisis. Instead, it was conjured, like the emperor's new clothes, as a critical input to make financial capture possible.

Finally, I conclude the book by proposing and describing some concrete ways to challenge the system of abstract domination of risk. I describe several proposals for challenging or undoing the stratification of interest rates produced by risk-based pricing. I also review the idea of "household unions" offered by Dick Bryan and Michael Rafferty (2018, 189), which they suggest might be able to extract political concessions from the power structures of modern finance by straining the flows of securitized debt and other payments that come out of households. These proposals are only first, grasping attempts to challenge financial capture by creating a politics of risk.

ONE

Capitalism as Capture

On its face, arbitrage—the act of buying and selling the same or similar things in different markets for different prices—is one of any number of financial trading strategies, and though it is relatively important in academic financial discourses, it should not merit the central position in a book on the relationship between culture and finance. Arbitrage's place of privilege makes sense only within a particular framework for understanding capitalism, one in which different forms of capitalism are organized around different—but isomorphic—processes of capturing value.

Capture

The framework I advance follows the work of J. K. Gibson-Graham (1996) and their project of decapitalizing big-C Capitalism. Their feminist economic deconstructionism declares that capitalism is more limited, more internally differentiated, and more specific than most political economic analyses give it credit for. In short, "There is no capitalism, only capitalisms" (247). I begin with the simple proposition that capitalism is defined not by class relations, production, or exploitation, but by a particular dynamic I call *capture*. I take the term from the work of Gilles Deleuze and Félix Guattari (2007), who describe an "apparatus of capture" as an assemblage that is made up of two operations, "direct comparison and monopolistic appropriation," which, taken together, yield a "difference or excess constitutive of profit" (441, 444). This movement can certainly be seen in the appropriation of the surplus value formula in Marx's (2003) *Capital*, which Deleuze and Guattari deploy as their first example. However, they multiply the number of processes to which they believe the label of capture can be applied, naming profit from the appropriation of surplus labor, ground rent, and taxation all as apparatuses of capture.

In addition to naming multiple apparatuses of capture, they also suggest that capture does not take advantage of existing differences, but rather that it is a process that produces the conditions for comparison where none existed before in order to exploit them. Elsewhere, I have described this inversion in the following way:

> Capture names a seemingly paradoxical operation in which the appropriation of a surplus (from some stock or totality) constitutes the very totality from which the surplus is appropriated. Capture works precisely by establishing the possibility of a difference (between the surplus and the stock), which enables the possibility of a comparison. And it is the comparison that enables the identification and appropriation of the surplus. Capture introduces difference into transformations of value by constituting both sides of the equation, so that the capture of the surplus (re)constitutes the stock from whence it came in the very act of capturing the Difference. (Grossberg et al. 2014, 324–25)

Capture is therefore a creative process, one that generates differential value measurements to allow for comparison and profit, but appears merely to find and exploit those differences.

Despite these insights, and each will be relied on in the elaboration of my argument, the notion of capture is not revolutionary. Instead, it is a derivative repurposing of the concept of surplus value appropriation. The choice to focus on the dynamic of that appropriation, and to center it with the term *capture*, is made strategically to open up and explore the possibility that the many "capitalisms" Gibson-Graham alerted us to are differentiated by distinct contexts or apparatuses of capture. For Marx (2003), exchange value is produced by abstract labor time measured quantitatively. The time spent by individual laborers creating use values is, in the process of capitalist production, transformed into abstract labor time. Quanta of abstract labor time are then crystallized in commodities that circulate. Through circulation, these quanta are compared to socially necessary quanta of abstract labor time (the labor time necessary to produce the products needed to reproduce laborers) such that a surplus of value produced by labor can be identified and captured by the capitalist (167, 299). The comparison of socially necessary labor time and surplus labor time does not exist prior to the conception of surplus value appropriation. The capture process makes these categories intelligible. In its absence, labor is merely "productive activity" and socially necessary labor time the time individuals spend provisioning themselves for survival (50). But, in industrial commodity production, surplus value capture creates a differentiation in the stock of productive activity and a comparison of total abstract labor time and socially necessary labor time that provides an excess or profit.

For Marx, capitalism *is* surplus value appropriation. But, taking capture as a framework, surplus value appropriation is but one form, allowing that capitalism may be internally differentiated by the existence of a number of forms of capture. It is this affordance of the term that leads me to adopt it. I have argued elsewhere, following Grossberg (2017), that theory should serve as "disposable tools, judged by their ability to help (re-)organize or re-narrate the overdetermined (and potentially chaotic) empirical realities of a context" (qtd. in Hardin 2017, 331). Instead of applying one's favorite theory to any given context, the researcher should engage in what I call "provisional framework building," which I define as mapping the "relations of a context, by deploying whatever theoretical resources might seem to work in whatever limited capacity—or finding/producing new theories or concepts when existing ones fail" (331). Capture is exactly that, a provisional framework for understanding finance where other theories have failed to adequately account for it.

Many have attempted to understand finance by analyzing it through Marx's framework of industrial surplus value appropriation (Duménil and Lévy 2011; Lapavitsas 2009; Vercellone 2010). But, because Marxist analyses center the industrial context, finance ends up being framed as either a parasite or in some way fictitious, belying its central and often determining effects. Marx declares: "Capitalist production is not merely the production of commodities, it is essentially the production of surplus-value. . . . That labourer *alone* is productive, who produces surplus-value for the capitalist, and thus works for the self-expansion of capital" (2003, 477; my emphasis). Later interpreters of Marx, such as Richard Wolff and Stephen Resnick (1987) and Harry Braverman (1998), reiterate the distinction.[1] For Marx, the credit system was also the domain of fictitious capital, since government bonds, other claims on debt, bills of exchange, and titles of ownership only represent claims on value but are not themselves values produced by labor (1991, 595).[2] He therefore designates the "national banks and the big moneylenders and usurers that surround them" in the credit system as a "class of parasites" (1991, 678).[3]

Even after the global financial crisis, many Marxist analyses have maintained these distinctions between the true heart of capitalism in the real, productive economy, and parasitic or fictitious finance. For example, in their 2011 explanation of the financial crisis, Gérard Duménil and Dominique Lévy ask, "Were the profits of the financial sector real profits?" (127) and answer themselves: "The analysis of the financial sector in the United States suggests . . . the formation of a strong bias toward fictitiousness, at least from the second half of the 1990s, with a dramatic expansion after 2000" (128). The financial sector produced fictitious profits through techniques like mark-to-market accounting that did not anchor the prices of financial securities to real production.[4]

Carlo Vercellone rejects the reading of the financial crisis that sees it as a spectacular buildup of fictitious capital. Instead, the crisis is indicative of a genuine crisis of "the *law of labor time value*" (2010, 86). Previously, capitalists organized production and reinvested surplus value in production; they were "agent[s] of production" (98). Today, capitalists appropriate value through a rentier logic that is facilitated by finance. But rent is "*a pure relation of distribution*" (98). Vercellone's argument places finance at the center of the new logic of capital, but then distances it from "real" production again by claiming that it is solely a parasitical drawing of rent from autonomous labor processes. In some ways, this reading is even more protective of the notion that finance cannot produce value than other Marxist readings. Financial rent has no "real function in the process of production" (102).

Geoff Mann's (2010b) article "Value after Lehman" offers a sophisticated rebuttal to such interpretations. He writes, "To see value as historically determinate is also to understand that—while value remains 'value,' the organising principle of capitalism—as capitalism changes, so too will the way in which value operates" (176). For Mann, the financial crisis reveals that "value as such has more recently escaped labour's bonds" (176). He challenges the notion that factories, machines, and land are "real" values whereas derivatives like those involved in the crisis are somehow fictitious by noting that the latter are "just another, albeit sophisticated and mystifying . . . commodity—one that the crisis has not so much exposed as fictional as rendered just plain valueless" (181). Mann suggests that financial activity need not be understood as unproductive, but goes further to suggest that taking finance seriously requires a reconceptualization of value. Value should not be defined as that which is produced by labor, but is "best understood as a form of social wealth constituted by a spatially and temporally generalizing social relation of equivalence and substitutability under, and specific to, capitalism" (177). That does not mean that abstract labor is no longer productive of value, as he notes: "Contemporary capital's power still lies to a significant extent in the expropriation of labour's surplus-product" (177). But other formations of the social relations that constitute value as such also exist. In particular, "the web of social relations" that constitutes finance is a source of value just as the social relations of labor are (181).

In the capture framework advanced here, I offer a fuller explanation of the "spatially and temporally generalizing social relation of equivalence and substitutability" that produces value (Mann 2010b, 177). Capture constitutes the value which it appropriates in its creative process of generating comparisons out of undifferentiated flows, in many different contexts. Marx looked behind the veil of exchange to see the hidden abode of production as the engine of capitalism (2003, 172). In the capture framework, there are many hidden abodes. Industrial production is one. Racial capitalism is, as I will shortly argue, another. The subject of this book, however, is the hidden abode of financial exchange, where arbitrage is the defining form of capture.[5]

Arbitrage consists of a trader identifying securities or commodities that are the same or sufficiently similar that they can be substituted for one another, buying the cheap one, and selling the more expensive one. Most economists and other social scientists describe arbitrage as a process of discovering arbitrage "opportunities" (Beunza and Stark 2004). However, in actuality, arbitrage is a process of creating a novel comparison that leads to monopolistic appropriation, that is, capture. I'll give an example to illustrate this point. Book publishers routinely produce two different editions of their textbooks; domestic textbooks are reproduced, with minor aesthetic changes, but identical text, for foreign markets. These international edition books are sold overseas, often at lower prices. The lower prices attached to international editions express the difference in contexts in which the books are used. U.S. higher education markets are characterized by inflated and ever-increasing prices for tuition, fees, and textbooks. In other markets, the cost of education is lower so international editions have lower prices that these other markets will bear. In other words, the two substantively similar kinds of textbooks circulate in different "regimes of value" (Appadurai 1986, 15). Arjun Appadurai defines "regimes of value" as "specific cultural and historical milieus . . . in which desire and demand, reciprocal sacrifice and power interact to create economic value in specific social situations" (4). In the early 2000s, a Thai college student named Supap Kirtsaeng financed his U.S. education and then some by reselling cheap international editions of textbooks in the United States (via eBay and other similar sites) for more than what they sold for in his native Thailand, but less than the cost of the standard domestic versions offered by publisher John Wiley and Sons.[6]

This arbitrage trade depended on Kirtsaeng intervening in two different markets, removing the international edition books from the context, or regime of value, in which they circulated, and transferring them into a different context to produce a comparison that allowed the differences in their prices to appear as an excess for appropriation. Before his intervention, the difference in their prices wasn't even really a difference, because each kind of book was firmly embedded in its own regime of value and its price reflected the conditions of that milieu. After his intervention, these books were placed in a relation that produced a comparison and an abstract difference in value much like the one between commodities and the wages paid to laborers who produce them.

John Wiley and Sons, Inc. sued Kirtsaeng, who appealed all the way to the Supreme Court, which ruled in 2013 that his arbitrage was legal. The court case showed that the comparison of commodities across contexts is a relationship that is not natural but must be established. Capture produces the conditions of comparison rather than merely finding them. In the case of *Kirtsaeng v. John Wiley and Sons, Inc.*, the success of the arbitrage rested not only on Kirtsaeng's actions, but on the complicity of the legal framework, which endorsed his comparison. The Supreme Court could have decided that Kirtsaeng did not have the right to resell the books, which would have meant a failure of capture to complete its operations.[7]

Arbitrage capture may appear fundamentally different from surplus value appropriation in which value is added through labor rather than switching markets, but several commentators have noted the similarities between the two. Economist Israel M. Kirzner (2008) has suggested that entrepreneurship—the quintessential case of the enterprising industrial capitalist—is actually arbitrage. He claims that an entrepreneur sees that, "by assembling available resources in an innovative, hitherto undreamt of fashion, and thus perhaps converting them into new, hitherto undreamt of products, he may be able (in the future) to sell output at prices that exceed the cost of that output to himself. In all its manifestations, entrepreneurship identifies arbitrage opportunities" (9). Similarly, Robert Meister makes the claim than an arbitrage trade is at the heart of the surplus labor value appropriation process described by Marx in *Capital*. He sees Marx's capital formula, M-C-M', as an "arbitrage opportunity in which an identical commodity has two different prices" (2016, 157). Surplus value is constituted precisely by the spread between the value of the products of labor power and the value of the wages paid to laborers.

Rather than claiming that all of capitalism is about arbitrage, I see these correspondences as evidence that capture is what different forms of capitalism have in common. Industrial capitalism looks like arbitrage because both are apparatuses of capture. However, the greatest payoff of the capture framework is not simply to show, as I will in the coming chapters, how futures trading, high frequency trading, mutual fund timing, and the trade in subprime mortgage-backed securities allow for the monopolistic appropriation of value. Marx spent but a single chapter—the first one—explaining the relatively simple calculation of surplus value in industrial capitalism. He spent the remainder of his three volumes as well as hundreds of pages in other works attempting to explain how this calculation was made possible, its conditions of possibility, and its possible conditions of overcoming. Similarly, the capture framework is an opening onto a set of questions, rather than an answer in itself. Chief among those questions is why? Why does monopolistic appropriation continue to occur if it immiserates those who are subject to its operations? In the industrial context, this question took the form of "Why does the proletariat accept the conditions of its own exploitation?" Marx answered this question in several ways, animating questions about politics, ideology, and domination that remain the subject of intense debate today. The same question must be asked of financial capitalism and financial capture through arbitrage. To do so, I take Moishe Postone's (1993) critique of Marx as a model.

Abstract Domination

Moishe Postone (1993) entered Marxian debates about labor and exploitation, arguing in *Time, Labor, and Social Domination* that the question of why the proletariat accepts its own exploitation is best answered by reframing labor to see it not as the transhistorical source of value—as traditional Marxists do—but a relation specific to capitalism. Traditional Marxists think that labor is, in all times and contexts, the source of wealth, and capitalism describes the process whereby that source of wealth is exploited. This leads to the notion that distributing the products of labor back to laborers would ameliorate the ills of capitalism. Postone disagrees, framing labor as a relation that defines the form of value specific only to capitalism and therefore is the "*ground* of domination" in capitalism (125). Postone explains that "labor itself constitutes a social mediation in lieu of overt social relations" (150), by which he means that within capitalism, social stratification and hierarchy do not determine who labors and how, but who labors and how determine social hierarchy. That is to say, the compulsion to labor in order to buy commodities is not "direct social domination," but instead "labor in capitalism gives rise to a social structure that dominates it" (159). Laborers accept the conditions of their own exploitation because the very category by which they understand their social world—labor—compels them to. Postone names this compulsion "abstract domination" and he characterizes it like this: "The abstract domination and the exploitation of labor characteristic of capitalism are grounded, ultimately, not in the appropriation of the surplus by the nonlaboring classes, but in the form of labor in capitalism. . . . Because the compulsion exerted is impersonal and 'objective,' it seems not to be social at all but 'natural.' . . . This structure is such that one's own needs, rather than the threat of force or other social sanctions, appear to be the source of such necessity. . . . one must labor to survive" (161). Ultimately, then, industrial capture is only possible because "this 'free' individual [the laborer] is confronted by a social universe of abstract objective constraints that function in a lawlike fashion" (163).

Postone's insights are a necessary corollary to the capture framework. Capture must be understood as the process by which value is appropriated in capitalism, but abstract domination is the ground on which that process functions. Postone, speaking only about the industrial apparatus of capture (production), nevertheless accurately describes the hand-in-glove relationship: "What characterizes capitalism is that, on a deep systemic level, production is not for the sake of consumption. Rather, it is driven, ultimately, by a system of abstract compulsions constituted by the double character of labor in capitalism, which posit production as its own goal" (1993, 184). Capture is the goal, and abstract domination the means to that end. Therefore, the capture framework is only complete when each apparatus of capture is understood to be reliant on a system of abstract domination built around a principle that presents as objective a number of social compulsions—a "quasi-objective form of social mediation"—whose primary purpose is to enable capture (5).

A short and speculative look at what others have called racial capitalism illustrates how Postone's notion of abstract domination can be fruitfully applied to other forms of capture. Jodi Melamed defines "racial capitalism" in the following way: "Capitalism is racial capitalism. Capital can only be capital when it is accumulating, and it can only accumulate by producing and moving through relations of severe inequality among human groups—capitalists with the means of production/workers without the means of subsistence, creditors/debtors, conquerors of land made property/the dispossessed and removed. These antinomies of accumulation require loss, disposability, and the unequal differentiation of human value, and racism enshrines the inequalities that capitalism requires" (2011, 77). In this formulation, the relationship between race and value is fundamental. Racism enshrines the differentiation that makes comparison with an excess possible. That is, race itself is a form of abstract domination. This can be traced at least as far back as the transatlantic slave trade.

The triangular trade in African slaves and the products of their labor is credited by Cedric Robinson (2000) as the seminal moment of the globalized modern economy. The apparatus of racial capture operating within it looks strikingly like Marx's industrial process, except one of the poles of comparison, the wage, is replaced by the cost of chattel slaves.[8] Slaves kidnapped in Africa and shipped to the New World produced tobacco, sugar, cotton, and other staple crops for more than one hundred years. European lords and eventually New World plantation owners purchased their labor at a fixed cost, like a capital input rather than a labor input, but the comparison was nearly the same. The value of the products created by the slaves was compared to the cost of purchasing and maintaining them as property, and the excess appropriated monopolistically. In slavery, capital produced commodities by swallowing the laboring bodies of slaves whole, without entertaining even a limited claim by them to the value produced. The appropriation of value enabled by this process enriched racial capitalists and contributed to the industrial and technological revolutions that define modern life today (Ott 2015). The system of abstract domination to which all members of the slave economy were condemned was not labor, but rather race itself.

Postone might disagree with describing racial slavery as capture, and race as a quasi-objective social mediation akin to labor, as he actually uses slavery as a counterexample to define the abstract domination of labor, describing it as "direct social domination" (1993, 159). He writes: "Non-alienated labor in societies in which a surplus exists and is expropriated by nonlaboring classes necessarily is bound to direct social domination" in the form of serfdom and slavery (160). In the most generous reading, one might credit this as a possibility in societies where slavery is not committed only along racial lines and where the appropriation of excess is not of such a great magnitude. Such may have been the case with some historical forms of slavery, including the early days of North American colonization when slaves of different origins, particularly people of Irish descent as well as indentured servants from several European countries, commingled with African slaves, and when people of African descent were also free and landholding members of society (Ott 2015; Robinson 2000). But the racial plantation slavery of the eighteenth and nineteenth centuries does not meet these tests. As sugar production grew and the concomitant demand for labor in the New World was met almost exclusively with kidnapped Africans (Robinson 2000, 117), race morphed from an ambiguous geographical category into the abstract principle that it is today. As Robinson explains, "the natural order of the races" was an ideology that was specifically created in order to justify the practice of racial slavery (76). The label *Negro* unlike *African* "suggested no situatedness in time, that is history, or space"; "the Negro had no civilization, no cultures, no religions, no history, no place, and finally, no humanity that might command consideration" (81).

The principle of race therefore produced a slavery in which "a marginally human group, a collection of things of convenience for use and/or eradication" could be bought specifically for the purposes of capture, no matter how at odds such a definition was with the abstract philosophical principles deployed to justify the creation of the United States of America as a nation, the religious principles of predominantly Christian slave masters, or the romantic sentiments of the nineteenth-century imagination (Robinson 2000, 81; Baucom 2005).[9] In other words, social racism became abstract race, and race functioned in the same way for slavery that abstract labor functioned for industrial production, that is, as a mystification of social relations that grounds the domination of capitalism while appearing to be a necessity. Race became a system of abstract domination that was "impersonal and 'objective,' it seems not to be social at all but 'natural'" (Postone 1993, 161). Just as labor transformed "productive activity" into the industrial production of capitalism (Marx 2003, 50), race transformed some bodies into capital inputs.[10]

The legal end of racial slavery in the United States did not end the social domination of race. Sharecropping, redlining, and numerous other examples of the differential economic treatment of Black Americans evidence the impact of the abstract domination of race after emancipation. In the twentieth century, the abstract domination of race morphed in specific ways that continue to justify capture. In what Melamed describes as the official state antiracisms that followed the "racial break" after World War II, "racialization converts the effects of differential value-making processes into categories of difference that make it possible to order, analyze, describe, and evaluate what emerges out of force relations as the permissible content of other domains of U.S. modernity (e.g., law, politics, and economy)" (Melamed 2011, 11). That is, the abstract domination of race in the post–World War II context maintains racial differentiation but tucks it neatly into new schemas of difference that obscure and justify it, such as "codes of patriotism, heteronormativity, cultural normativity and those signifying class or professional status" (13). The production of supposedly neutral credit scores that nonetheless reflect differential exploitation and racial segregation is a key example of this logic, which I examine in more detail in chapter 6. Melamed also describes the value constituting work that this form of racialization accomplishes: "Racial knowledges . . . do not just arrange human beings along a pregiven scale of value. Instead, they are at once productive and symptomatic of the total value making (such as political value and economic value)" (11). Her work reinforces the framing of abstract domination, and shows how that domination morphs over time to continue to justify the comparisons needed for capture, even as conceptions and treatments of race change.

Similarly, Keeanga-Yamahtta Taylor (2019) has illustrated the way that race structured housing markets in the United States during the twentieth century. Against the notion that civil rights and fair credit legislation in the 1960s and 1970s undid the harms of redlining and racial exclusion of Black homebuyers, Taylor illustrates the way that government negligence and the profit motive in the real estate industry combined to produce "predatory inclusion" of Black borrowers. Programs like the Federal Housing Authority's Section 235 low-income lending program did not open the American Dream of homeownership to low-income urban borrowers. Rather, it plugged these borrowers into a profit-making scheme led by criminal HUD and FHA officials and real estate agents, in which dilapidated homes were sold at greatly inflated prices to poor borrowers. These homes saddled Black borrowers with expensive repairs or barely habitable homes, which quickly led to foreclosures. What should have been segregation-ending policies that lifted Black borrowers into the middle class through property ownership deepened Black urban poverty. It was not pure greed or overt racism but the complex interaction of these and other factors that conspired to ensure that Black borrowers were only "granted access to conventional real estate practices and mortgage financing . . . on more expensive and comparatively unequal terms" (5). Thus, the 1960s and 1970s do not represent a radical shift in the relationship between consumer debt and race. Instead, "From racial zoning to restricted covenants to LICs [land installment contracts] to FHA-backed mortgages to the subprime mortgage loan, the U.S. housing industry has sought to exploit and financially benefit from the public perceptions of racial difference" (261).

Laura Pulido (2016) argues that race is "a constituent logic of capitalism" in modern contexts such as the Flint water crisis (7). She explains that racism marks some peoples and places for abandonment by capital and elevates the rights of municipal bondholders above the lives of Black residents. For Pulido, "the devaluation of Black (and other nonwhite) bodies . . . creates a landscape of differential value which can be harnessed in diverse ways to facilitate the accumulation of more power and profit" (1). Within the capture framework, the precise dynamics of this devaluation become visible. The abstract domination of race indeed produces differential value for Black bodies as opposed to white. Under slavery, those bodies were valued solely economically while white bodies were allowed to retain extra-economic values—of humanity—that Black bodies were not. In contemporary capitalism, racialized "surplus people and places" produce a new comparison, between the cost and profit potential of reproducing some people and places and not others (8). In Flint, the cost of reproducing a Black city through taxation and state investment was deemed too high. Instead, the city financed social services by issuing bonds, and then when a conflict emerged between the ability to provide clean drinking water to residents or repay bondholders, the latter won out. The rights of bondholders were elevated over the lives of residents, creating a race-secured comparison between the risk of default if Black bodies were valued, and the much lower default risk when they are not, yielding a surplus profit to bondholders. In this example, the abstract domination specific to racial capitalism fuses with another system of abstract domination: risk.

Risk

Risk is the abstract principle that organizes and directs financial flows of value to capture through arbitrage. Like race and labor, its definition is historically contingent and socially powerful, compelling individuals as if by necessity.[11] The history of the financial concept of risk, as well as the history of individual investing and borrowing, reveal the way this form of abstract domination functions.

In 1921 Frank Knight famously distinguished uncertainty from risk, defining the latter as "an uncertainty which can by any method be reduced to an objective, quantitatively determinant probability" (qtd. in Rubenstein 2006, 50). Peter L. Bernstein describes Knight as a cynic, who "harbored too many doubts about the rationality and consistency of human beings to believe that measuring their behavior would produce anything of value" (1998, 219). For Knight, entrepreneurial profit was derived from uncertainty, not risk.[12] Also in 1921, in *A Treatise on Probability*, John Maynard Keynes emphasized the importance of differentiating between things that could be predicted with probabilities and those human events that could not (Chappe et al. 2013). Like Knight, "Keynes rejected theories that ignored uncertainty," basing his injunction for "a more active role for the government" in part, on the notion that it needed to "reduce uncertainties abroad in the economy" (Bernstein 1998, 228). However, despite Knight's and Keynes's early skepticism of probability, financial economics became progressively more concerned with the measurement of risk throughout the twentieth century. Ironically, contra Knight's schema, these risk calculations are the necessary condition of comparison that allow for profits to be had through arbitrage capture in finance today.

Financial securities are stripped-down representations of value: a share of stock is a claim to a portion of a company's profits, a bond is an entitlement to future repayment, and an option is the right to purchase something of value at a future date. As such, securities are defined in financial economics along exactly two vectors: risk and return. The foundational Capital Assets Pricing Model (CAPM) calculates the expected return of a stock as a function of its beta, or its correlation to the market, that is, systematic risk. Other formulas for pricing bonds, options, and more all deliver price as a function of some term (often an interest rate) that represents risk. Since arbitrage is necessarily the buying and selling of the same or similar goods, and risk defines similarity in financial securities, arbitrage between different securities can occur when two securities of similar risk trade at different prices. It can also occur when securities with the same return have different risk measurements, as in the case study of this book: the transformation of pools of mortgages into mortgage-backed securities. The same mortgages populate both pools, but due to the supposed diversification effects of the securitization process, mortgage-backed securities were given credit ratings above the aggregate rating of their underlying pool. The arbitrage trade this allowed drove demand for subprime mortgages and spurred the housing bubble. All of this, however, presupposes that risk is an objective measurement that can establish the comparison of likeness or difference. As recently as 1944, risk was not considered to be an objective fact. In that year, John von Neumann and Oskar Morgenstern's *Theory of Games and Economic Behavior* characterized risk as the *subjective* probabilities individuals assign to potential outcomes. In their work, individuals' expected utility was modulated by their attitude toward risk, not by an objective measurement of it.

Just a decade later, Harry Markowitz defined those formerly subjective probabilities as the historical variance of the stock's price to establish his foundational portfolio selection formula (Rubenstein 2006). Markowitz was on the cutting edge of the mathematization of finance that would facilitate the slippage between the idea that risk was a construction of subjective probabilities and the notion that risk was objective and measurable. The objectified form of risk pioneered in Markowitz's portfolio selection was further enshrined in the Capital Assets Pricing Model (CAPM). Following Markowitz, the beta used to estimate a stock's correlation to the market in the CAPM is calculated using historical variance as the measure of risk, further solidifying the notion that risk was objective and measurable.

In 1973, the Black-Scholes-Merton (BSM) options pricing formula brought the objectification of risk to its apotheosis by providing a measure of risk as an output of the formula when applied to existing option prices (Black and Scholes 1973; Merton 1973).[13] The formula was originally constructed to use the historical variance of the underlying stock, like Markowitz's formula, as an input to provide the correct price of an option to buy or sell that stock. Quickly, however, economists discovered that the formula could be used in reverse, inputting market prices and backing out the measure of risk they implied. This *implied volatility* term would seem to be a measure of stock price change in the next moment in the future, that is, a true prediction of risk in the present, without reference to the past (Latané and Rendleman 1976). The convention for traders became, and remains, to quote the implied volatility rather than the option price. This term presents itself as an empirical fact that doesn't require grounding in the past.

Today, risk measurements play key roles in financial policy and regulation. The Basel Accords on international banking standards sets minimum capital requirements using credit rating agency ratings, which can also be found in Securities and Exchange Commission regulations and in internal guidance for large institutional investors like pension funds (Benmelech and Dlugosz 2009). Traders use risk measurements like betas and credit ratings to determine how to hedge their portfolios. And corporations of all sorts use "value at risk" estimates to comply with various regulations and agreements about their financial viability ("Value at Risk" 2019). These measurements are precisely what is compared in arbitrage trades to determine the excess. Risk measurements grease the rails of financial flows, offering probabilistic calculations to enable individuals and firms to make investing and trading decisions. But, in specific cases, risk measurements also make particular arbitrage trades possible. As I show in chapter 5, differences in prices of raw subprime mortgage loans and mortgage-backed securities constructed on them constituted the surplus of arbitrage profits on mortgage securitization in the run-up to the financial crisis. Securitizers justified this difference in prices by arguing that the mortgage-backed securities were less risky than the raw mortgages that underlay them, due to diversification and other credit enhancements like overcollateralization. However, as the financial crisis made clear, defaults on mortgages flowed through to the mortgage-backed securities despite this supposed difference. In other words, the very idea that the risk of each set of securities could be measured, and those measurements compared to establish a surplus, enabled the entire apparatus of capture based on subprime mortgage securitization to function.

Beyond the confines of financial markets themselves, popular discourses and practices of financial risk drive individuals to put their money and their futures at risk through investing and borrowing, both of which provide the raw material for arbitrage capture. Popular financial advice has come to fill the void in material guarantees of education and retirement previously provided by the welfare state. There is a new common sense that one must manage her credit score and put her money to work in order to secure her future; 529 college savings plans and individual retirement accounts (IRAS) are held up as solutions to the problems of runaway tuition costs, the disappearance of traditional pensions, and the perpetual crisis of Social Security. Even the flatlining of wages for low- and middle-income workers over the last fifty years is framed as a failure of individuals to take advantage of finance. A recent eTrade commercial illustrates the point. A curly-haired young man dances excitedly on the deck of a megayacht, clearly living his best life. Then, the eTrade logo appears alongside text that announces "The dumbest guy in high school just got a boat." The man we now know to be "the dumbest guy in high school" jumps into the crystal blue water, and the ad goes in for the kill, ending with "Don't get mad. Get eTrade" ("ETRADE—Yacht Life").[14] The implication is clear. If you aren't buying a boat, it's not because of the political alliance between neoliberalism and neoconservativism that has produced economic policy changes to shift risk from corporations and the government to individuals and nuclear families, widening income inequality to the same levels as the Gilded Age (Cooper 2017; Sommeiller and Price 2018). It's because you aren't trading stocks with eTrade.

The reality is of course much bleaker than popular discourses make it appear. During the stagflation years in the 1970s, Americans turned from insured savings accounts to money market and brokerage accounts to avoid the depreciation effects of high inflation (Nocera 1994). Even after the Volcker Shock tamed inflation, investing is framed as the rational way to protect savings from inflation and grow funds to meet future demands. As I have argued elsewhere, professional consumer financial discourses and technologies like retirement savings calculators that visualize future returns serve to assure investors that markets offer inflation-beating returns in the long run (Hardin 2014). Professional assurances conspire with threats to the Social Security system, the erosion of traditional pensions, and the increasing cost of higher education to make it seem like common sense that investing is the only right way to save money for the future, even if, in reality, investing is necessarily risky and investors may need the money precisely when the market is down. In other words, just like with the abstract domination of labor, "the compulsion exerted is impersonal and 'objective,' it seems not to be social at all but 'natural.' . . . This structure is such that one's own needs, rather than the threat of force or other social sanctions, appear to be the source of such necessity" (Postone 1993, 161). Long-term individual investors provide fertile ground for professional traders to produce comparisons and capture excesses as profits, as I will illustrate in chapter 4.

Everyday borrowing is the other side of the risk coin. Contemporary U.S. consumer culture has for the last fifty years squeezed individuals between the injunction to purchase more and more stuff essential to social life—homes, cars, computers, phones, clothes, furniture, gadgets, and the like—and increasing real costs of homeownership, rent, higher education, healthcare, and childcare. Consumer credit fills the gap between the two, allowing people to continue to increase consumption even while wages languish. Homeownership has been a special site of everyday borrowing. Eighty years of government intervention to increase mortgage borrowing

combined with cultural transformations in the meaning of homeownership to create the home as an intense location of both cultural and economic speculation in the years before the financial crisis. As Fiona Allon
(2010) explains, before the financial crisis, "one of the primary expectations to emerge was that by embracing financial market risk, and successfully calculating and managing that risk, owning a home would provide
a store of housing wealth that could be depended on not only to finance
consumption in the present but to provide social and economic security
over the life course" (375).

In this context, it is unsurprising that 80 percent of Americans live in
debt (*Complex Story* 2015). And the other 20 percent are either too poor to
borrow or too rich to need to. Americans in debt risk their futures by betting that debt-funded expenditures will elevate their position and income,
but the possibility that the debt will have overwhelming negative impacts
is great. Over 8 million homes were foreclosed on during the financial
crisis, saddling borrowers with both immediate and lasting material and
financial hardships (Calhoun 2018). Other forms of debt are risky for
borrowers as well. Children of parents with unsecured debt have more
socioemotional problems (Dwyer 2018). For adults, "high relative debt
(debt-to-asset ratio), . . . was associated with higher perceived stress and
depression and worse self-reported general health, even when accounting
for life-course health and economic conditions and other indices of current socioeconomic position" (Sweet et al. 2013, 98). Student loan debt
"fuels economic, gender, and racial inequality, inhibits asset accumulation, accelerates wealth gaps, and carves out a generational divide that,
even in the best of circumstances, will take decades to erase" (Frotman
2018, 823).

Over the last half century, the way consumer credit is lent has also
changed. In the 1960s and 1970s, credit underwriting was transformed by
computerization, allowing for the calculation and scoring of the creditworthiness of potential buyers (Langley 2008). Today, one's credit score is one
of the most important factors in social and economic mobility, determining
the ability to rent an apartment, get a job, and, of course, borrow money.
For the latter purpose, that score determines not just if one can get credit,
but how much it will cost as well, in the form of the interest rate. Through
the principle of "risk-based pricing," credit products are more expensive for
people with lower, that is, riskier, credit scores (Langley 2008, 150).

These interest rates are the basis for arbitrage in debt securities. Financial firms bundle consumer debts—mortgages, car loans, credit card

receivables, and student loans—into bond-like securities that investors can purchase and from which arbitrageurs can appropriate an excess. The higher the interest rate, the more excess is available. Therefore, lending to those who are deemed riskier by their credit scores, but who can nonetheless afford to pay back their high interest loans, is the sweet spot for finance. Lenders prefer debtors who are just risky enough. This is why credit card lenders famously refer to those borrowers who always pay their balances in full as "deadbeats" (Manning 2000, 5). These borrowers offer no spread, and therefore no excess.

Postone argues that capitalism "is characterized by *personal indepen-dence* in the framework of a system of *objective ... dependence*," that is, people appear to be individually free, but are compelled by apparently objective needs to do the thing—labor—that allows capitalism to function and appropriation of surplus to take place (1993, 125). Value-producing labor is therefore, for Postone, both a historically contingent phenomenon specific to capitalism and a form of abstract domination. Exploitation is not the greatest evil of capitalism; that "productive activity" is condemned to serve as value-producing labor is the true scandal. Risk—as the principle that compels everyday investment, structures everyday borrowing, and makes arbitrage possible—is the "quasi-objective form of social mediation" in financial capitalism (5). Postone states that, "on a deep systemic level, production is not for the sake of consumption. Rather, it is driven, ultimately, by a system of abstract compulsions ... which posit production as its own goal" (184). This statement can be reformulated in finance: On a deep systemic level, risk doesn't exist to facilitate future returns on investment or debt-based consumption but rather to organize a set of compulsions that posit *arbitrage* as its own goal.

Politics

The documentary *Inside Job* (2011), which endeavors to explain the causes and impacts of the financial crisis, was released three months after the Dodd-Frank Wall Street Reform and Consumer Protection Act was passed. It chronicles the history of deregulation and derivative-based financial trading in a muckraking style that focuses on exposing and humiliating individual executives, regulators, and Wall Street defenders in one-on-one interviews. Interviews with critics who had tried to get people to listen to reason before the crisis reinforce the line between the good guys and the bad guys. In addition, the film contrasts the outrageous conspicuous consumption of traders and golden parachute–clad executives with the plight of hardworking Americans forced into tent cities by the recession, and bailouts for big banks with the lack of government assistance offered to homeowners facing foreclosure or laid-off workers. The resulting narrative suggests that a conspiracy of rich, white financial professionals and government officials perpetrated a heist on ordinary Americans. Greed is the ultimate driver of these processes, leading financial lobbyists to pollute government, financial board members to pollute economics, and financial trading to pollute the real economy. *Inside Job* ends by arguing that federal prosecutors have passed up a multitude of ripe opportunities to prosecute the villains of this story, and that "the men and institutions that caused the crisis are still in power, and that needs to change." However, the amount of space given to contemplating how such a change might play out is strikingly small. No suggestions of specific reforms are made, no heroes provided. In fact, exactly one sentence is devoted to discussing the change. It is the final sentence of the film: "It won't be easy, but some things are worth fighting for."

Inside Job tells the technical story of the crisis well and highlights the complexities of the entrenched power of finance in the twenty-first century. But it also serves as an exemplar of the popular common sense about postcrisis Wall Street. That common sense combines two contradictory story lines, which run through most critiques of finance. On the one hand, finance wins. Finance is utterly powerful, utterly entrenched, utterly wealthy, and it has so thoroughly captured government, the economy, and even individuals—reliant as they must now be on debt and investing—that it cannot possibly be challenged.[15] On the other hand, it is obvious that finance must be fought, that the Wall Street traders—with their Ivy League educations; endless appetites for hookers, drugs, and vacation houses; and remorseless avoidance of penalties for inflicting widespread harm and suffering—are the enemy, whether individually, as a class, or as a system. The real harm caused by the financial crisis makes this view seem not only common sense, but the only moral choice. But the nature of that fight is almost always left entirely unspecified. Sometimes, as in *Inside Job*, a vague notion of reform is suggested. However, concrete ideas on what kind of reform might actually have the desired effect of making finance fairer or less vampiric are harder to come by.

Together, the omnipotence of finance and the moral requirement to fight it produce a "structure of feeling" that is long on rage, and short on specifics (Williams 1977). There may be no better example of this than the Occupy Wall Street (ows) movement that emerged in the fall of 2011. It was the physical embodiment of the desire to rage against all the villains so artfully painted in *Inside Job*. In a reflection of the ethos of finance itself, ows drew the antagonism between the bad guys and the good guys with statistics, impugning the "1 percent" for their wealth, power, and disregard for democracy, while asserting the rights and dignity of the "99 percent" ("Occupy Wall Street"). The movement took aim at many of the same ills depicted in *Inside Job*, including the complicity of regulators and the illiberalism of lobbying. Its "occupy" strategy was meant to disrupt the business-as-usual of Wall Street, and then of entrenched government and corporate power more generally. Ultimately, ows attempted to reclaim power by the only means left to the thoroughly outgunned (in many cases, literally) majority: mere presence.[16]

Ten years on, it appears that ows impacted political discourse by bringing the issues of income inequality and corporate power more into the mainstream than in the naive years before the crisis (Levitin 2015). But, as a movement aimed specifically at finance, even its organizers agree that it was a failure (White 2015). That failure would seem to reinforce the commonsense narrative that Wall Street is omnipotent, that despite the masses finally taking to the streets—as they are so often maligned for failing to do—ows didn't change finance one wit. While ows posted a list of demands and spun off initiatives like the Strike Debt movement, which is not without its own successes, it did not prompt any change in the power differential between the 1 percent and the 99 percent ("Strike Debt!"). With the election of Donald Trump in 2016, the revolving door between finance, lobbyists, and government went into overdrive. Trump continued the bipartisan historical trend of appointing former Goldman Sachs employees to high-ranking positions, but also appointed more donors, many with little qualifying experience, than previous presidents as well. The 1 percent seems to have been enriched, in both wealth and power, in the time since ows took to the streets.

During the same period, academics suggested some frameworks for thinking about a political response to the crisis. However, many embodied the same commonsense narrative of entrenched power and the need to fight it. For example, in *The Violence of Financial Capitalism*, Christian Marazzi (2011) advances the thesis that finance produces a new commons which it then divides, privatizes, and expels inhabitants from, through the artificial creation of scarcity—a dynamic he likens to the reemergence of primitive accumulation.[17] In this dynamic, which he terms "biocapital-ism," value is not extracted solely from laborers anymore; finance extracts "surplus-value by pursuing citizen-laborers in every moment of theirs lives" (49, 55). The image of a stalking vampire squid, reinforced by the invocation of violence in the book's title, makes clear that this state of af-fairs represents a complete capture of power by financial capitalism and also that things need to change. While Marazzi advocates New Deal–style social welfare reform, he doesn't grapple with the political reality of how such a plan might actually be accomplished.

John Bellamy Foster and Fred Magdoff's (2009) *The Great Financial Crisis* has a more neutral title, but it is accompanied by cover art that jibes perfectly with the commonsense narrative of finance: a balding, musta-chioed, Depression-era banker with the hooves, ears, tail, and horns of a bull is washed in a reddish tint (suggesting those horns might be more representative of the state of his soul than his opinion of the market); with a pipe in his mouth, he is blowing bubbles inscribed with "INFLATED VAL-UES" that the little guys—men and women in more austere Depression-era dress—frantically grab for. Behind the cover, Foster and Magdoff offer their "stagnation thesis," that the increasing dominance of finance is capitalism's response to its own stagnation beginning in the 1970s (100). Financial markets offered a home to surplus capital produced in mono-poly capitalism. Following stagnation and without productive activity to direct it toward, interest-bearing debt and speculative bubbles are where capital now goes. The result is a "deep-seated, irreversible economic im-passe," the effects of which we are now living through (83).

Foster and Magdoff trumpet their own predictive prowess in having called the financial crisis before it happened, making their prediction for what will happen after the crisis seem both certain and devastating: "The prognosis then is that the economy, even after the immediate devaluation crisis is stabilized, will at best be characterized for some time by minimal growth and by high unemployment, underemployment, and excess ca-pacity" (2009, 133). When, in the final few pages of the book, they turn self-reflexively to discussing "*political* economy," they, like Marazzi, suggest New Deal–style social welfare as a solution, calling for "a mass social and economic upsurge" to accomplish it (139). But in what can only be read as a melancholic admittance of defeat, they, like *Inside Job*, devote a single vague sentence to the issue of *how* to transform financial capitalism: "If such elementary prerequisites of any decent future look impossible under the present system, then the people should take it into their own hands to create a new society" (139). Like the reminder that "some things are worth fighting for" (*Inside Job* 2011), the injunction to "take things into their own hands" can only serve to highlight the fact that short of what would almost certainly be, in this time of militarized policing, a bloody and ineffectual attempt at revolution, there are no effective options for strategically challenging finance. The impotence of raging against the machine is, ultimately, as starkly evident as the omnipotence of finance is.

Both popular and intellectual political challenges to finance have lacked a vantage from which to see it as contingent and vulnerable to changes in the system of abstract domination that undergirds it. None of these challenges has homed in on arbitrage as the key dynamic, nor seen risk itself as a problem, much less *the* problem, with finance. Financial capitalism built on arbitrage capture has a long history, which I chart in the coming chapters. Arbitrage is at least as old as the early days of mercantile capitalism, when money changers found that trading currencies could provide profits. But its ascendance to political power is relatively recent and our understanding of it is in its infancy. Likewise, many commentators, especially within economics and economic sociology, have claimed that erroneous risk measurements contributed to the housing bubble and its crash. But there is no mention of, much less a consensus around, the idea that risk is a construct which imposes itself on us in order to compel our participation within a system that dominates us. I argue precisely this, that arbitrage and risk should be subject to critical scrutiny and political calculation; that just as the racial wealth gap and the minimum wage are targets of political challenge, credit scores should be also. Challenging the widespread acceptance that risk is a natural fact, which can be measured, and that those measurements constitute objective—neutral, apolitical—justifications for many of the very conditions that impoverish people, is a prerequisite for meaningful action to change how finance operates. The remaining chapters unpack these notions, and begin the work of framing them not only as analytical tools for understanding finance, but as strategic targets for change.

TWO

Arbitrage in Theory

The definition of arbitrage proffered by financial economics affords it a central position within finance theory as the guarantor of market efficiency. In this role, arbitrage actually fulfills a number of disciplinary and imaginary functions. For one, in financial economics, it actually appears most prominently in its absence, as the "no-arbitrage condition," which is used as a test that prices are efficient, that is, correct (Bodie et al. 2009, 325). But more broadly, market efficiency is a moral imperative within the neoliberal vision of the market as a better information processor than any central planning agency could be (Hayek 1945). Since arbitrage is the mechanism that ensures efficiency, it actually enacts a kind of wish fulfillment within the neoliberal imaginary.[1] It is thus unsurprising that, in addition to occupying a place of privilege in financial modeling, arbitrage is also framed in broader popular and regulatory discourses as a benevolent force ensuring fair pricing for all market participants. In this chapter, I unpack arbitrage's paradoxical role in finance theory, its theoretical role in market efficiency and the broader neoliberal conception of free markets, and the consequences of policymakers, regulators, and judges accepting the benevolent definition of arbitrage proffered by financial economics. In short, I tell the story of the *benevolent-efficiency narrative* of arbitrage to show that, through it, financial economics justifies and protects the practice of arbitrage from the kind of critical scrutiny it deserves.

The Origins of Arbitrage in Financial Economics

The term *arbitrage* was probably not used until the eighteenth century, although the concept of buying and selling at differing prices is much older. According to Geoffrey Poitras (2010), the term *arbitrio* may have been used to describe the "arbitration of exchange rates for different currencies observed at the medieval fairs" as far back as the twelfth century (8). At these fairs, "a representative body composed of recognized merchant bankers" would discuss and vote on exchange rates of various currencies for that specific fair (2). The modern word *arbitrage* shares a root with arbitrate, arbitration, and the Latin *arbitrari* meaning "to give judgment," all of which are freighted with notions of justice and fairness (69). For the deliberative process of setting exchange rates at medieval fairs that seems reasonable. But, as I elaborate in this chapter, despite contemporary arbitrage being quite a different affair, these meanings remain woven into the conceptual role it plays within financial economics.

While the concept of arbitrage is quite old, its role in contemporary financial economics is newer. This is because contemporary financial economics is itself quite new. Prior to the 1950s, finance was studied from an "institutionalist" perspective (MacKenzie 2006, 38). The discipline of finance taught "a mix of common sense, judgment, and tradition that had strikingly little to do with economics" (Fox 2009, 78). Mark Rubenstein (2006) goes so far as to designate the time before 1950 as the "Ancient Period." From the 1950s onward, however, the study of finance became more oriented toward economic modeling and increased in mathematical sophistication. The "fundamental analysis" that dominated in the Ancient Period, in which the "intrinsic value" of a stock was determined based on qualitative and quantitative evaluation of a business and the macroeconomic factors that might impact it, gave way to simpler and more mathematically elegant models based on assumptions of perfect information and rational decision-making among market participants (Bryan and Rafferty 2013, 10).[2]

Franco Modigliani and Merton Miller's (1958) article "The Cost of Capital, Corporation Finance and the Theory of Investment" is one of the earliest examples of this emergent financial economics and is also the first time that the concept of arbitrage is deployed as a key part of a financial model.[3] In their article, Modigliani and Miller apply economic reasoning to a common problem in corporate finance: whether a firm should finance a new project by issuing stock or borrowing through bonds. This decision about the "capital structure" of the firm was examined in great contextual detail in the Ancient Period. Management-based finance professors focused not only on the cost of each strategy but also on the attitudes of investors toward stocks after the 1929 crash and the negative impact on a firm's image if it held too much debt (MacKenzie 2006). Modigliani and Miller eschewed all these considerations for a single "simplifying assumption" (Fox 2009, 75) that "investors . . . prefer more wealth to less" (Modigliani and Miller 1958, 269n11). Using this assumption, they set up a logical, rather than empirical or descriptive, argument that the capital structure of a firm was irrelevant. In their model, the firm's total market value wouldn't change depending on whether it financed a project with stock, bonds, or any mix of the two.

To prove their argument, Modigliani and Miller proposed two identical firms that made different decisions about how to fund their next (identical) projects. One firm funded it with an issuance of stock, and the other with both stock and debt. They argued that, because the firms are identical and undertaking the same project, they both offer investors access to equal future streams of profits. Therefore, if, hypothetically, the second firm's stock value were to drop—say, because investors view debt negatively— rational traders would see that the two firms were offering the same future profit stream for different (stock) prices, and would perform arbitrage. Because those rational traders value more wealth over all else, they would buy the low-cost firm and sell the high-cost firm, gaining a profit from the transaction. If the firms were truly equivalent, the investors would still expect the same future profit stream from their investments in the new firm, but would have made an arbitrage profit to boot. According to Modigliani and Miller, "The exchange would therefore be advantageous to the investor quite independently of his attitudes towards risk" (1958, 269). In other words, investors' irrational fears about stocks or debt would be effectively trumped by their desire for profit.

The actions of these rational, arbitraging investors would eventually— through the mechanism of supply and demand—make the prices of the two firms become the same. The higher-value firm being sold would experience excess supply, lowering its price, while the lower-value firm being bought would experience excess demand, raising its price.[4] Modigliani and Miller's "simplifying assumption" about investors' preference for wealth, coupled with the expectation that traders would always engage in arbitrage if they could, meant that even if capital structure impacted the value of a firm initially, arbitrage would always quickly correct such irrationality.[5]

This reasoning, that prices would conform to rational expectations because, if they did not, arbitrage would occur and force them into those expectations, would become the dominant underlying basis for financial pricing theories in the years following Modigliani and Miller's paper. It eventually gained the name of the "no-arbitrage condition," which proposes that securities will have prices that do not allow arbitrage to take place (Bodie et al. 2009, 325). The immediate corollary to this condition is that if prices ever do allow arbitrage, investors will immediately undertake it and—through the dynamics of supply and demand—prices will then snap back to their "no-arbitrage" levels.

The no-arbitrage condition gave rise to an entirely new set of financial models focused on the pricing of derivatives, beginning with the famed Black-Scholes-Merton (BSM) options pricing formula published by Fischer Black and Myron Scholes in 1973. Before the derivation of this formula, warrants and options were notoriously difficult to price and options markets didn't exhibit any sort of rational consistency (MacKenzie 2006). Black and Scholes originally attempted to price options using the Capital Assets Pricing Model (CAPM)—which was a non-arbitrage-based formula that gives the return on a stock as the function of its correlation to market risk (Fox 2009). Robert Merton argued against basing option prices on CAPM and instead performed a mathematical derivation that gives the price of an option as a function of the current stock price, the strike (exercise) price of the option, the "risk-free" interest rate (the rate on safest borrowing, usually U.S. Treasury bonds), the time to expiration of the option, and the volatility (the historical standard deviation or square root of variance) of the underlying stock (Bodie et al. 2009, 729).

Like Modigliani and Miller's capital structure argument, the proof of the BSM formula relied on an arbitrage argument. Option prices must conform to the BSM price because, if they don't, an arbitrage opportunity would exist. An investor could produce a "replicating portfolio" consisting of fractions of the underlying stock and risk-free borrowing that would give the exact same payoff as the option (Derman 2013, 11). The option price must therefore equal the cost of producing such a portfolio, or else arbitrage would ensue. Once the formula was developed and accepted, it became a functional guide to arbitraging options prices, and thus induced the very mechanism for making itself true.[6] That is, the BSM appears to be the inception point of what could be called an academic-to-market pipeline by which financial economists identify theoretical arbitrage opportunities and publish journal articles describing them and then market participants undertake those arbitrages. When Black began to publish price sheets list-ing the BSM theoretical prices and volatility estimates for different options, traders used them "in the practice of arbitrage . . . and the effects of that arbitrage seem to have been to move patterns of prices toward the postu-lates of the model," thus removing the arbitrage opportunity and profiting traders who undertook it (MacKenzie 2006, 166).[7]

It is hard to overstate the importance of BSM for establishing the no-arbitrage condition as the gold standard for financial price determination. It allowed for the pricing of many forms of derivatives, from futures and options to more exotic financial securities whose values are "derived" from that of another. The derivation of that value occurs through the replicat-ing portfolio technique underlying BSM. The pricing of futures contracts (and their over-the-counter cousins, forwards) is today taught in business schools through the use of the no-arbitrage condition.[8] The futures price of a particular commodity must be equal to the cost of borrowing money to buy the commodity today and hold it until the date of the expiration of the future. *If it is not* (the hallmark of the no-arbitrage logic), arbitrageurs would buy the lower priced of the two strategies (either entering a futures contract or borrowing to buy and hold the underlying commodity) and sell the higher-priced strategy, netting a profit from the difference. In this case, the futures contract can be simulated with a replicating portfolio in the form of borrowing to buy and hold the commodity at current prices. The futures price must be the price of the replicating strategy or else arbi-trage would occur and eventually, force the price to that level anyway.

It is assumed that, with enough time and trade volume, the forces of supply and demand will raise the price of the cheap asset that traders want to buy, and lower the price of the expensive asset that traders prefer to sell. Eventually, this will bring the prices of these economically equivalent as-sets together at a point of parity (see figures 2.1 and 2.2), a process called convergence.

The Limits to Arbitrage

In his book, *Understanding Arbitrage*, Randall S. Billingsley defines arbi-trage in this way, capturing many of the finer details explained in financial economic textbooks: "Arbitrage is the process of buying assets in one mar-ket and selling them in another to profit from unjustifiable price differences. 'True' arbitrage is both riskless and self-financing" (2006, 2). The second

Arbitrage Opportunity

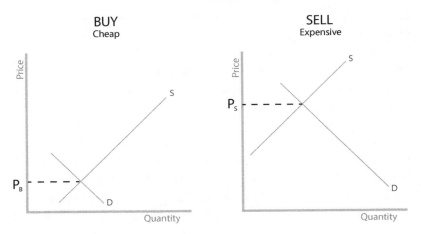

Convergence

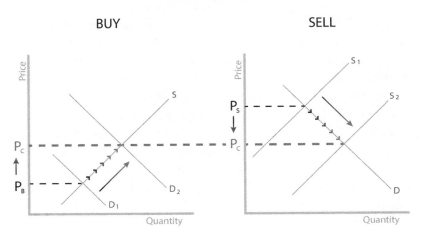

FIGURES 2.1 AND 2.2 The Law of One Price is theoretically ensured by the actions of arbitrageurs and the dynamics of supply and demand. As arbitrageurs buy the cheap good, they increase demand ($D_1 \rightarrow D_2$). As they sell the expensive good, they increase supply ($S_1 \rightarrow S_2$). Prices thereby converge to P_C.

clause implicitly announces some controversy over the definition. "True," offered in scare quotes, points to the fact that the arbitrage described by textbooks is somehow purer than some other kinds of trading that are also (perhaps questionably) called arbitrage. True arbitrage must be "riskless" in the sense that it is a trade based on an erroneous disparity in price and not based on a speculative investment that might or might not pay off, and also "self-financing" in that it is done with borrowed money rather than the trader's own capital. In a sense, this little "true" in Billingsley's definition announces that there is something like pure arbitrage in the abstract that exists in financial formulas, and something else, some imperfect copy or copies out there in the world that we might call *arbitrage in real life*.

This distinction isn't surprising. Milton Friedman (1962) famously argued that unrealistic assumptions do not matter, as long as the predictive power of the model is clear. Financial models are often based on wildly unrealistic assumptions of perfect frictionless markets, while real markets contain all sorts of limits that make the models poor or totally incongruous representations. What's more, financial economists don't believe that the frictionless worlds of their models are actually real. For example, Donald MacKenzie (2006) reports that Modigliani was somewhat uncomfortable with the unrealistic assumptions underlying his joint work with Miller on the irrelevance of capital structure from the beginning. Similarly, in her ethnography of students in a Master of Computational Finance program at a business school in New York, Stephanie Russell-Kraft reports that her informants were well aware that financial models in general and the no-arbitrage condition in particular are "all wrong" (2013, 39).

In the 1980s and 1990s, behavioral economists went a step further than acknowledging the unrealistic assumptions of financial models and began documenting the "limits to arbitrage" (Bodie et al. 2009, 389). This literature compiled a long list of factors that prevent arbitrage opportunities from being taken up in real life. They argue that, unlike the frictionless, riskless arbitrage of financial economics, real-world arbitrage is necessarily risky. Theoretical arbitrage will always pay off as, in theory, convergence between the prices of equivalent securities is ensured. In practice, though, Andrei Shleifer and Robert W. Vishny note that "in most real-world situations arbitrageurs also face some long-run fundamental risk" (1997, 49).

The "limits to arbitrage" literature supposes that the necessary risks of real-life trading can complicate attempts at arbitrage or prevent them altogether, which results in a number of persistent anomalies in which real-life financial prices fail to converge. For example, De Long et al. (1990) discuss the effects of noise traders—irrational traders who may be unjustifiably bullish or bearish on certain securities. Arbitrageurs who try to profit from the resulting mispricing of assets can only do so if prices eventually start to move back toward rational values, that is, the values they should have under the no-arbitrage condition. Economic models assume that arbitrageurs have an infinite time horizon, but noise trading may cause mispricing to persist so long that traders must exit their positions before prices converge. Shleifer and Vishny (1997) explain that firms that perform arbitrage with investors' money face limits as well. Self-financed arbitrage—done with borrowed money and/or borrowed securities (short selling)—faces the risk of margin calls. Traders may borrow money to buy into a position, or borrow securities to sell, but they must also post a minimum amount of capital in a margin account according to federal law. Diverging arbitrage trades may require additional margin deposits. Hedge fund managers will likely set limits on how much they are willing to deposit on diverging trades. Traders using investors' money may encounter resistance from their investors if they must ask again and again for additional margin deposits on a trade. The diverging trade will appear to investors like a loss and they may respond by pulling money out instead of investing more.

Denis Gromb and Dimitri Vayanos (2010) point out that even traders using their own capital might not survive such a trade. Without infinite capital, they may not be able to meet margin requirements, even if they are certain the arbitrage will eventually pay off. They also list persistent anomalies such as the value of stocks going up when they are added to prominent market indices and the value of stocks sold by distressed mutual funds going down. The limits to arbitrage have prevented arbitrageurs from completely eliminating the anomalies.

The limits to arbitrage literature reflects the fact that financial economists are well aware of the unrealistic assumptions underlying the no-arbitrage condition and that such arguments don't fit real-world circumstances. However, the banner under which this research is carried out ("limits to arbitrage") suggests that, despite issues with arbitrage, it cannot be scrapped completely as an explanation of pricing or as a goal of financial trading. Rather than studying the prices of securities in different markets as the outcomes of a complicated interplay of factors in divergent "regimes of value" (Appadurai 1986), behavioral economists assume a priori that markets should be efficient and could be, if theoretical arbitrage could be perfectly enacted in real life. This perspective highlights the normative role of arbitrage in visions of how the world should function. Efficiency—a connected single market in which all goods trade at equivalent (right) prices—is accepted as a moral good, and arbitrage as the vehicle for achieving it. By identifying the factors that hinder or prevent arbitrage, this literature shifts the blame for the unrealistic assumptions underlying financial models from financial economics to irrational investors and regulators who are not conforming to the efficiency that should exist. Arbitrage is held up as a self-evident goal and it is the responsibility of these irrational actors to conform to the models, not the models to conform to actual market practices. As I explain below, this is because arbitrage is central not just to financial economics, but to the broader neoliberal ideology that holds efficient markets up as guarantors of social freedom.

Arbitrage and/as Freedom

The no-arbitrage condition formally pioneered by Modigliani and Miller and turbocharged in the BSM formula is the only theory in financial economics that has risen to the status of law. The "Law of One Price" restates the no-arbitrage condition in the following way: "If two assets are equivalent in all economically relative respects, then they should have the same market prices" (Bodie et al. 2009, 325).[9] The word *should* here indicates something important about the nature of this law. The fact is that similar or even the same securities do trade at different prices in different markets for any number of contextual reasons ("animal spirits" [Keynes 1936] or "irrational exuberance" [Greenspan 1996]) are ways economists have attempted to explain this fact), meaning that the Law of One Price does not always, or even frequently, hold. The Law of One Price is not, therefore, a law in the scientific sense, that is, a fact of nature that has been confirmed by repeated observation. Instead, it is more like the juridical laws of nation-states in that it is a moral imperative that requires executive enforcement. Market traders are the police who carry out that enforcement. As one textbook puts it, "The Law of One Price is enforced by arbitrageurs: if they observe violation of the law, they will engage in arbitrage activity . . . until the arbitrage opportunity is eliminated," that is, until the excess supply of the expensive asset and the excess demand for the cheap asset produced by the arbitrage trades force their prices to converge, just as Modigliani and Miller proposed (Bodie et al. 2009, 325).

The arbitrage reasoning of the Law of One Price is the proof of the famed "efficient market hypothesis" published by Eugene Fama in 1970.

The efficient market hypothesis states that all available information is already reflected in equilibrium prices. This boils down to the point that traders act rationally on information individually, leading to an aggregate system in which all information is reflected. The mechanism by which information about whether securities are the same or similar is transmuted into prices is arbitrage. According to the Law of One Price, arbitrage keeps prices in parity across markets and between similar securities, making markets efficient and fair for all traders.

But the notion that markets are efficient is not a neutral, scientific hypothesis. If markets can be made to be efficient, if they can be pushed into the idealized state of processing all available information, specific moral goods will be achieved. The entire edifice of neoliberal ideology constructed by the Mont Pelerin Society revolves around the notion that economic planning is inferior to market order because, as Friedrich von Hayek argued, the latter is by definition able coordinate the needs and resources of humans better than any "one single mind" ever could (1945, 526). Hayek specifically holds up arbitrage as an example of the kind of activity that contributes to the coordinating function of the market. Together, the "shipper," the "real estate agent," and "the arbitrageur who gains from local differences of commodity prices, are all performing eminently useful functions based on special knowledge of circumstances of the fleeting moment not known to others" (522). These individuals with special, fleeting knowledge continually adjust the "one price" of any commodity in real time, processing all information better than any central planner could (526).

In *The Road to Serfdom*, Hayek ([1944] 2007) specifically held market coordination up as a cure for the creeping threats of socialism and fascism, which in opposition to popular wisdom, he saw as two sides of the same central planning coin. Keith Tribe (2009) characterizes the argument like this: "What distinguishes neoliberalism from classical liberalism is the inversion of the relationship between politics and economics. Arguments for liberty become economic rather than political, identifying the impersonality of market forces as the chief means for securing popular welfare and personal liberty. This was essentially Hayek's argument—that in a society where decision-making was largely centralized, welfare and freedom would be undermined" (76).

The idea that the market is "an information processor more powerful than any human brain" (Mirowski 2009, 435) was adopted as a central doctrine of what Dieter Plehwe describes as the "neoliberal thought collective"—a group including Friedrich Hayek, Ludwig von Mises, Milton Friedman, and Karl Popper (2009, 6). The group began meeting in Mont Pelerin, Switzerland, in 1947 with the aim of "learn[ing] how to effectively oppose what they summarily described as collectivism and socialism" (2009, 6). According to Philip Mirowski (2009), the collective "succeeded in constructing and deploying elaborate social machinery designed to collect, create, debate, disseminate, and mobilize neoliberal ideas" aimed at "winning over intellectuals and opinion leaders of future generations" (432, 431). Mirowski attributes much of what we think of as neoliberal changes to government policy and institutions to the epistemological project of the neoliberal thought collective and the think tanks and lobbying groups it spun out.

This machinery influenced financial economics from the 1950s on, as the Mont Pelerin Society and the influential Chicago School of economics "were joined at the hip from birth" (Van Horn and Mirowski 2009, 159). The economic theories that have ended up positioning arbitrage at the center of a normative vision of what the market ought to be were likely influenced if not directly inspired by this fusion. Read through the doctrines of the neoliberal thought collective, arbitrage is the linchpin not just of financial economics, but of the larger neoliberal project. As the guarantor of efficient market functioning that, in the neoliberal imagination, is the only cure for socialist inefficiency and fascist domination, arbitrage is indeed a moral imperative.

The Benevolent-Efficiency Narrative

The enforcers of the Law of One Price—and therefore, in neoliberal doctrine, the crusaders for freedom from illiberal social organization—are rational traders undertaking arbitrage for profit. The Law of One Price often fails. Prices do not stay in parity as it suggests; but traders in their pursuit of monopolistically appropriated—captured—profits are assumed to be performing a social good on a grand scale. This framing is evident in financial and behavioral economics, but it also circulates in discourses outside of economics, where arbitrage is framed as a kind of public service, and arbitrageurs as friendly police officers who keep markets fair by assuring that all traders pay the same price for economically equivalent assets. This benevolent-efficiency narrative of arbitrage is evident in the realms of sociological research, financial trading itself, and law and regulation.

In the first decade of the 2000s, several economic sociologists began to focus on arbitrage as an object of study. Donald MacKenzie's (2003) study of arbitrage trading at Long Term Capital Management (LTCM) focused on the supply and demand mechanism of buying low and selling high that should push disparate prices toward one another. According to MacKenzie, because financial theory suggests that prices should be in parity, and arbitrage trading actually causes that theory to become correct, arbitrage trading is usually "performative" of financial economics. He writes: "To the extent that arbitrageurs can eliminate the price discrepancies that finance theory helps them to identify, they thereby render the theory performative: price patterns in the markets become as described by the theory" (351).

MacKenzie (2003) goes on to show that in 1998 LTCM lost more than $2 billion because, despite the economic definition that sees arbitrage as riskless, its trades eventually failed to make a profit as prices diverged and investors fled the trade. However, this case study does not convince MacKenzie that the benevolent-efficiency narrative is incorrect. Instead, he uses it to suggest that the limits to arbitrage literature should include social problems as one of the things that can disrupt the arbitrage mechanism. According to MacKenzie, the LTCM's arbitrage trade would have worked except that sociological processes like imitation intervened. MacKenzie writes: "The key risks may be 'social' risks from patterns of interaction within the financial markets, rather than shocks from the 'real economy' or from events" (373). Like the behavioral economists' limits to arbitrage literature, MacKenzie takes for granted that arbitrage is about bringing prices into parity and only qualifies this by suggesting that sociological processes may sometimes interfere.

Ian Hardie more straightforwardly defends "the place of arbitrage within efficient markets theory" (2004, 244). Hardie rebukes MacKenzie's and other sociologists' use of the term *arbitrage* to include trades that do not strictly conform to the arbitrage conditions outlined in economic textbooks. In 2006, in a collaboration with Daniel Beunza and MacKenzie, Hardie softens his position on pure arbitrage. The three elaborate a new project for economic sociology, which they term *material sociology of arbitrage* (Beunza et al. 2006, 722). In setting up the project, they claim that "arbitrage constitutes markets" (722) by bringing prices in different markets into parity at a "world price" (723). Their main intervention, then, is not to critique the benevolent-efficiency narrative, but to argue that real-world arbitrage "can properly be understood only if it is grasped in its full materiality and sociality," something they hope to undertake in "collaboration between financial economists" and researchers in other disciplines (741). Such a collaboration would likely have to assume the benevolent-efficiency interpretation of arbitrage to be possible.

Researchers are not the only ones who draw on this dominant narrative about arbitrage; traders also deploy it as a way to defend their actions and fend off regulation. Hirokazu Miyazaki writes that, when index arbitrage came under scrutiny as a possible cause of the 1990 stock crash in Japan, "Sekai arbitrageurs . . . asserted that arbitrage performed the important economic function of linking the cash and futures markets so that investors might use the futures markets for hedging" (2007, 404). Without arbitrageurs enforcing the Law of One Price, hedging one's investments would be impossible. They defended their trading practices by citing the benevolent outcome of ensuring parity between the two markets, and therefore fair access to securities for all traders.

High-frequency traders make similar arguments in defense of their practices. High-frequency trading (HFT) often involves forms of arbitrage, exploiting differences in pricing over very short intervals of time. An industry group representing HFT firms repeated a common refrain in 2014 that HFT "lowered costs, tightened spreads and added liquidity" to markets.[10] High-frequency traders claim that by initiating many orders quickly over time, investors encounter a more liquid market with fewer trading costs, that is, efficiency is increased. In a letter to the editor of the *Wall Street Journal*, Tom Joyce, CEO of an HFT firm, explained that "retail investors today benefit from the lowest trading costs and the highest execution quality in history."[11] Many critics of HFT point out that practices like "front running"—trading on orders before other market participants are aware of them—qualify as predatory and even blame the 2010 "Flash Crash" on HFT.[12] Yet, like other arbitrageurs, high-frequency traders fall back on the economist-certified benevolent-efficiency narrative of their activity to imply that, like referees in sporting events, their arbitrage activities are keeping markets fair for everyone.[13]

Regulators, policymakers, and even judges use the benevolent-efficiency narrative of arbitrage in matter-of-fact ways that reinforce and justify arbitrage in practice. A case heard by the Seventh Circuit Court of Appeals in 1995 demonstrates this point.[14] A Chicago market-maker firm, Scattered Corporation, short sold millions of shares of the steel manufacturing corporation Ling-Temco-Vought ahead of their scheduled reorganization. The reorganization would, according to public documents, lower the price of existing stock to pennies a share. Yet buyers did not carefully dissect the reorganization plan and therefore were happy to buy the stock from Scattered at much higher prices. Scattered sold 170 million shares of stock that netted them $25 million in profit. The buyers filed suit alleging market manipulation, but the lawsuit was dismissed by Judge Richard Posner.[15] In his decision, Posner perfectly outlined the benevolent-efficiency narrative of arbitrage:

> The name for what Scattered did is not market manipulation, but arbitrage. Arbitrageurs are traders who identify and eliminate disparities between price and value. . . . By doing this, arbitrageurs promote the convergence of market and economic values that we suggested was the central objective of securities regulation. Consider a case in which the identical stock is selling for different prices on two exchanges at the same time. Since the value is the same, the prices should be the same. By buying stock on the exchange where the price is lower and reselling it on the other exchange, the arbitrageur brings about a convergence of price with value. . . . Arbitrage is not market manipulation. The opposite of a practice that creates artificial prices, it eliminates artificial price differences.[16]

In another example, Securities and Exchange (SEC) division director Paul Roye explained that the SEC was working on a new sort of investment known as electronically traded funds (ETFs) which, like index funds, would allow traders to buy and sell a pooled group of bonds. The regulatory body needed to figure out how to "achieve enough transparency of the Fund's portfolio to permit the arbitrage discipline to function so as to keep the market price of shares close to the fund's net asset value" (2001). This reference to "arbitrage discipline" pulls directly from the benevolent-efficiency narrative.[17] Roye takes for granted that, through arbitrage, the prices of EFTs will be kept in parity with the value of the bonds that make up a fund. Sixteen years later, in a speech on electronically traded products (ETP)—the broader category that now includes ETFs and other kinds of similar products—SEC commissioner Michael S. Piwowar (2017) included an even more textbooklike explanation of arbitrage:

> Arbitrage trading ensures that the prices at which ETPs trade reflect the intrinsic value of the product's underlying assets or the benchmark it tracks. If the price of the ETP deviates too much from the price of the underlying basket of securities, this creates an arbitrage opportunity. For example, large broker-dealers could buy the cheap ETP and short sell the underlying

basket. The broker-dealer would then deliver the ETP shares to the fund in exchange for the underlying basket, which would then be used to close out the short sale. This process helps ensure that ETPs trade near their intrinsic value—a benefit to all investors.

The implication of this speech is clear. Arbitrage keeps prices near their intrinsic value, so it is a positive force in the market that even removes the need for outside regulation.

The benevolent-efficiency narrative of arbitrage is unrealistic because, as I have shown, persistent anomalies often prevent arbitrage from carrying out its parity-enforcing role. But that is not its greatest flaw. More important is that, within the narrative, the issue of *profit* is distorted. Economists acknowledge that arbitrage yields a profit, but within their narrative, that profit is the incentive and reward for carrying out the benevolent function of ensuring efficient markets for all participants. The profit gained by traders who engage in theoretical arbitrage is an error, a mark of inefficiency. It isn't exploitation or theft, it's a penny on the ground, free for the taking, which happens to go to those doing us all the service of cleaning up the markets. When behavioral economists point out the limits to arbitrage— the fact that it does not exist in the idealized form found in financial textbooks, and the fact that efficiency is not always achieved by it—they fail to pose the important follow-up question of what that failure means for how we understand arbitrage profit. Where does that profit come from? When arbitrageurs win, who loses? What kind of system is required for arbitrage profit making to take place, and what kind of system does the practice of arbitrage reinforce?

Financial economists do not ask or answer these questions, because the benevolent-efficiency narrative forecloses them. Therefore, the system of financial economics that produces the discourse within which arbitrage is both central and present in its theoretical absence, can be read as a successful system of apologism for financial capture. It is a way of explaining arbitrage without ever pulling back the curtain to examine the true "hidden abode" of value production. It is not that the benevolent-efficiency narrative is false or mistaken—at times arbitrage does cause prices to converge—it's that this narrative directs our attention to those times and the beneficial effects in those cases, and away from a systematic analysis of the other consequence of arbitrage, the profit. Financial economics promotes claims about the practice of arbitrage and policy recommendations to allow and even foster it that have dramatic real-life effects. The economic justification of theoretical arbitrage enables arbitrage in real life.

Arbitrage has been practiced in U.S. financial markets since at least the nineteenth century. Anecdotal evidence suggests that it has grown as the dominant form of trading since the 1980s, when arbitrage pricing models in financial economics came into full flower.[18] Over the same period of time that arbitrage has flourished as a technique of financial profit making, income inequality in the United States has grown exponentially, with those in the financial services sector and CEOs leading the expansion at the top (Mishel and Sabadish 2012). Therefore, understanding arbitrage is not only important for understanding finance, but also for understanding broader shifts in capitalist dynamics today.

Statistics on arbitrage are not readily available because arbitrage is a secretive practice. Profiting from arbitrage depends on the arbitrageur having knowledge of a price disparity that others do not. For this reason, firms don't release details about their arbitrage trades. Firms invest in, nurture, and guard their arbitrage operations—and are well rewarded for it—because it is the mode of capitalist capture in the financial context. What the consequences of real-life arbitrage are for markets, citizens, and society is an important, unanswered question. Financial economics provides an effective justification and defense of financial capture by way of a theoretical notion of arbitrage, but it doesn't give anything like an account or study of arbitrage in real life. To understand finance, its role within capitalism, and the way that capture takes place within it, such a study is sorely needed.

THREE

Arbitrage IRL

In 1896, economist Henry Crosby Emery offered an account of speculation in the United States in which he made a particularly insightful distinction between what he called "time-speculation" or "time-dealings" on the
one hand, and "place-speculation" on the other (137). For Emery, time-
speculation was a form of financial trading that attempted to profit from
changes in the price of financial securities with the use of futures contracts.
Time-speculation was carried out "when an anticipated difference in the
present and future prices of the commodity in question leaves room for a
possible profit" (33). So, for example, if a speculator believes that the future
price of gold will be higher than it is today, he can buy futures at a price
close to the current or spot price. If his conjecture proves correct, he can
net a profit of the difference between the low price the futures contract
allows him to pay and the high price for which he can then immediately
sell gold back. Of course, he might also find that prices are lower in the
future, meaning his speculation cost him rather than enriched him. Time-
speculation is unlike investing in that the trader is not buying gold and
waiting for it to appreciate, but betting on potential appreciation with a
futures contract.

Emery contrasted this time-speculation with "place-speculation," which
he defined in this way: "to buy where goods were cheap, and to sell where
goods were dear." Place-speculation is "trader's business," the exchange of
goods across space that merchants had undertaken for centuries. Emery
argued that "place-speculation . . . was not separable from ordinary trade

under the earlier conditions of imperfect and uncertain means of communication." However, when communication technologies (in his time, the telegraph and the telephone) became so advanced that "the prices in both the selling and the buying markets are known at the same moment," place-speculation ceased being only the province of the merchant, and became a form of financial profit-making quite distinct from time-speculation. Emery notes that "such business is today known as 'arbitrage'" (1896, 137).

For Emery, arbitrage differs from both time-speculation and the buying and selling that constitute ordinary merchant trade by the instantaneity of price discovery. Arbitrage becomes possible when traders can know the price in buying and selling markets "at the same moment" (1896, 137). Emery's explanation anticipates the financial economic definition of arbitrage that would follow his work more than fifty years later in that it gestures toward the notion that the potential profit to arbitrage can be known and captured with certainty. Unlike the risk that the merchant undertakes when he begins a long journey, in which the demand for goods or the price they will bear could shift so much as to erase his profit, Emery's arbitrageur knows, and acts on, the disparity in prices instantaneously. No shifts in price over time can threaten the trade. In other words, what makes arbitrage arbitrage and not merchant trading is that the former is riskless (Billingsley 2006, 2). As I explained in the last chapter, risklessness is part of the definition of ideal arbitrage. But even though behavioral economists have enumerated multiple factors that prevent true riskless arbitrage, the notion that arbitrage is somehow more certain than other forms of trading is a key part of the way that economists both new and old distinguish it from other forms of trade.

The *Oxford Dictionary of Finance and Banking* puts it like this: Arbitrage is "the entering into a set of financial obligations to obtain profits *with no risk,* usually by taking advantage of differences in interest rates, exchange rates, or commodity prices between one market and another . . . an arbitrageur will only switch from one market to another if the rates or *prices in both markets are known.*"[1] Today, traders use microwave and laser signals rather than the telegraph and telephone to know and act on prices before they change. So the difference between arbitrage and other forms of financial trading rests on a particular relationship to time and space. What we might think of as traditional investing—buying a share of stock or investing in a startup directly—requires an openness to time; the hope is that the capital contributed will grow in value over time. Investing does not yield instant profit, but instead requires time to pass. What Emery calls time-speculation, the use of derivatives to secure future profits, also requires this openness in that profit will accrue at the expiration of a futures contract. Both investing and time-speculation seek to profit from the unfolding of time.[2]

In principle, arbitrage doesn't require the unfolding of time, and in fact, in its purest form, it negates time completely. The ideal arbitrage of financial economics relies on instantaneous price discovery and instantaneous trading to secure profit in the present or at a particular delivery date regardless of price changes that might occur before that time. In fact, arbitrage profits would be endangered if time were allowed to pass between the moment that a price discrepancy is identified and each leg—buying and selling—of the trade is executed. Instead of openness to time, instantaneity is key to arbitrage profit because any temporal separation between calculating profit and actualizing that profit introduces the possibility that the conditions on which the calculation of profit is based may change. The same is true for the temporal separation of buying and selling. If one leg of the trade is entered into at a time prior to the second, the price of the latter asset may change disadvantageously.

The problem, of course, is that true instantaneity isn't actually possible. Even the fastest computer programmed with an algorithm to identify arbitrage opportunities and act on them immediately is still limited by the speed at which electronic signals can travel across space. Running algorithms requires tiny increments of time, and fiber-optic cable only transmits signals at about two-thirds the speed of light.[3] Microwave and laser signals travel even faster, but they aren't truly instantaneous. True instantaneity of execution and simultaneity of both legs of arbitrage is an absolute limit point that existing technology cannot achieve. Space is never fully annihilated. The only trades that are possible involve some temporal interval and some spatial separation, and therefore, in the purest sense, some degree of uncertainty.

In this chapter, I argue that instantaneity matters not because it is actually achievable in arbitrage trading, but because real-life arbitrage is best defined as those kinds of financial trading in which buying and selling instantaneously is *simulated* through a number of different techniques. Arbitrage profit comes from buying cheap and selling dear, but it must be secured through different techniques that attempt to insure against the possibility that prices will change with the uncertain unfolding of time. Specifically, arbitrageurs use either financial derivatives contracts, or what I call *network differentials* to simulate instantaneity and create the most certain profit outcome possible. Financial contracts stabilize prices over time through legally binding agreement, which limits the contingency of unfolding time by fixing a price over a set period, thus negating the effects of supply and demand. Even if buying and selling activity changes prices over time, the contracts ensure that arbitrage can be carried out at a later date using the original contracted price, thus simulating instantaneity.

Network differentials are advantages in communication—especially the speed and spatial connectedness of arbitrageurs' communication networks—that allow some to profit more securely from arbitrage than others.[4] Arbitrage requires communication. Arbitrageurs, whether of currencies in the eighteenth century or equities in the twenty-first-century stock market, must learn of price discrepancies between markets, and trades depend on the transportation of goods and/or communication of trading signals for the purposes of buying and selling. Arbitrage thus relies on the differential ability of some arbitrageurs to communicate through their networks better and faster than others. Network differentials reduce the time lag between calculating a potential arbitrage profit and trading on it, and between each leg of a trade. Therefore, arbitrageurs who exploit network differentials profit before or at the expense of slower arbitrageurs. The use of price-stabilizing derivatives contracts and network differentials are ways that traders can execute arbitrage as if simultaneously, thus simulating the theoretical conditions of true arbitrage in real life.

Three important insights become clear when defining real-life arbitrage as buying and selling under conditions of simulated instantaneity. First, since in some cases trading on a price disparity can cause those prices to converge—via the mechanism of supply and demand—the first trader to notice and execute an arbitrage opportunity may be the only one to profit from it.[5] Add to this the fact that arbitrage trades often require network differentials in the form of technological or structural advantages and it becomes clear that, far from a benevolent mechanism producing fair, efficient prices for all, arbitrage involves a highly competitive arms race to secure the best network differentials with which to execute arbitrage trades before others.

Second, because arbitrage delivers profit to those who can find—or, in the capture framework, construct—price differences, efficient markets where prices are in stable parity are actually the enemy of arbitrage traders! Arbitrageurs do not want efficient markets; they want changing prices that can be mined for even the smallest and most fleeting differences. When markets grow more efficient with stable, fair prices, arbitrage traders will pursue new models, software, or technology to try to find smaller price disparities that previously couldn't be perceived or acted on, or identify new equivalences between securities that they believe should have price parity but do not.

Finally, since arbitrage is actually about exploiting proprietary advantages, the public rarely sees it. But when the public does become aware of arbitrage trading—usually in moments of crisis—it often responds with anger and condemnation. When arbitrage trading becomes evident, it is usually decried as unfair and exploitative. Other traders who cannot match the network differentials of the best arbitrageurs call foul, and commentators point to its negative effects on markets and investors, contradicting the benevolent-efficiency narrative that researchers, arbitrageurs, and regulators sometimes cite.

In what follows, I examine a number of historical examples of real-life arbitrage that came under public scrutiny to illustrate each of these arguments. I discuss the way that simulated instantaneity, both through price stabilizing contracts and network differentials, enables arbitrage. I also examine the competitive arms race to find ever newer and more advantageous network differentials. Finally, I recount the public outcry that ensued when arbitrage became visible, drawing a sharp contrast between the benevolent-efficiency narrative of arbitrage in financial economics and arbitrage in real life.

The Historical Origins of Simulated Instantaneity: Postlethwayt's Arbitrage

According to finance professor and economic historian Geoffrey Poitras, the first documented instance of something like modern arbitrage can be found in eighteenth-century merchant manuals, under the name "arbitration of exchange" (2010, 2). Poitras recounts an arbitrage described in a 1751 merchant manual authored by Malachy Postlethwayt. The manual provides calculations of "arbitrated rates" between London, Paris, and Amsterdam (6). Arbitrated rates were the rates of exchange that established parity between all three currencies, such that the same amount of currency would be gained from exchanging London sterling directly for French crowns as would making a "triangular" trade where London sterling is first converted to Amsterdam groats and then Amsterdam groats to Paris crowns (3).

However, Postlethwayt also showed how to make an arbitrage profit if "the actual exchange rate is above or below the arbitrated rate" (Poitras 2010, 6). In one example, the Amsterdam-Paris exchange rate is significantly higher than the arbitrated rate. Therefore, the arbitrageur could carry out the following trade. First, he sells a bill of exchange in London for repayment in Paris and receives sterling in exchange. He uses these funds to buy a bill of exchange in London repayable in Amsterdam in groats. The arbitrageur then travels to Amsterdam and receives groats. He transports these to Paris and exchanges them for crowns to cover the original bill sold. This trade would net a self-financing arbitrage profit if the Amsterdam-Paris exchange rate were high enough to more than cover the transport costs involved.

Postlethwayt's arbitrage relies on the most sophisticated financial trading technology of the time, the bill of exchange. Bills were a feature of early banking, originating in Islamic trade and entering Europe around the thirteenth century. They functioned like a hybrid of a personal check and modern paper money at a time when metal coins were the predominant form of currency. One banker would issue a note to a customer, drawn on or referencing the funds in his account. This bill would instruct a second banker in a different location to repay the face value of the bill at a future date, often to a different payee, in a different currency, and at a specified rate of exchange. The customer could then present the bill to the payee as payment, without having to carry and deliver metal coins (Ingham 2004).

Over time, like modern currency, bills of exchange became fully transferable. Instead of being linked only to the original account holder and payee, they circulated as proto–paper currency with large, fixed face values.[6] Eventually, bills facilitated currency exchange, as they could be traded for coins or bills in other currencies instead of just commodities. When states began to establish "sovereign monetary spaces," bills were the blueprint for state-backed credit money, which was basically a system of bills of exchange issued against the tax-collecting state rather than individuals (Ingham 2004, 100). But it was their role in currency exchange that made them an important early tool of arbitrage.

In Postlethwayt's example, the arbitrageur uses perhaps the very first technology for simulating instantaneity, the bill of exchange, to reduce the uncertainty that exchange rates might change during the time it would take the trader to travel between Paris, Amsterdam, and London. Bills of exchange were contracts that fixed exchange rates during the duration of the bill and across the physical space over which they were transported. They therefore allowed arbitrageurs to lock in profits, effectively simulating instantaneity by artificially negating the possibility of change over time. This mirrors the effectivity of contemporary financial contracts such as futures and options. Because bills of exchange necessarily specified a rate of exchange at which they could be used as payment or exchanged for coins, they stabilized the exchange rate that could have otherwise fluctuated over the intervening time that an arbitrageur had to travel from one location to another. This price stabilization was key to early triangular arbitrage.

But bills of exchange fit into both the price-stabilizing contract and network differential categories because they also produced positive network differentials for those who used them in the place of coins. As James Carey explains, prior to the invention of the telegraph, "transportation and communication were inseparably linked" (1992, 15). Hence, trading relied on transportation networks. One could not call or click to secure trades. Coins had to be physically transported between markets. Although today we might equate coins and bills as forms of currency, bills of exchange were a revolutionary development that reconfigured early transport-communication networks by replacing physical coinage with smaller, lighter, easy to conceal paper slips, thus alleviating some of the dangers of transporting metal coins. As Paul Einzig points out, during the eighteenth century, physical coinage had to be moved "under the guard of a heavily armed convoy" (1970, 67). Arbitrageurs who used bills instead of coins could travel faster, avoid the cost of the armed convoy, and draw far less attention to the value they carried, reducing the danger of robbery. Therefore, bills of exchange created a network differential between those who used bills and those who had to transport physical coins.

At this point, when communication was synonymous with transport, bills were more clearly a technology for overcoming both time *and* space. Arbitrage was, at this time, more clearly "place-speculation" in Emery's terms. By securing a rate of exchange in advance, bills evidenced Marx's famous aphorism about capitalism's "annihilation of space by time" (Marx 1973, 524). In the passage where Marx uses the phrase, he continues to explain that this annihilation is accomplished when "the direct product can be realized in distant markets in mass quantities in proportion to reductions in the transport costs," which is precisely what bills accomplished (524). Indeed, network differentials specifically involve relative advantages in traversing space, whether that space is covered by wagon transport or microwave transmission.

However, advantages in communication for the purposes of arbitrage are not just about who has the fastest communication technologies. As will become clear below, relative advantages of network connectivity can sometimes trump absolute advantages of speed.[7] Network differentials describe the relative advantages of successful arbitrageurs within a particular technological context. The network differential in Postlethwayt's eighteenth-century arbitrage created by bills of exchange made arbitrage cheaper, easier, and faster for the carriers of bills. In some cases, this may have amounted to a reduction in costs that quite literally produced an arbitrage profit where before none existed. If the potential profit from a triangular trade between Paris, Amsterdam, and London was less than the cost of an armed convoy to transport coinage, the use of bills of exchange may have allowed for the calculation of an arbitrage profit previously unavailable due to that cost. Network differentials that allow some arbitrageurs to simulate instantaneity often also reduce costs and thus increase, or even produce new, arbitrage profits. Importantly, because network differentials are used to secure arbitrage profits, and arbitrage is the highest goal of financial trading, network differentials tend to even out over time. As more participants use a network to execute trades, the advantages of early adopters are wiped out.

By the mid-eighteenth century, the diffusion of bills of exchange and advances in banking evened out the advantageous network differentials of early arbitrageurs. When multiple merchants traded using bills of exchange, supply and demand brought prices more closely into parity, just as the financial economic definition of arbitrage says it would. After all, Postlethwayt's explanation of arbitrage is found in a manual. Over time, merchants undertook trades as he instructed, and the relative advantages of bills of exchange became common knowledge. This evening out of network differentials is a story that recurs over and over in the history of arbitrage. It is an event that both reduces arbitrage opportunities in the present, and spurs arbitrageurs to go hunting for new advantages via better network technologies. Just as traders who began to use bills of exchange were able to capture profits that previously would have been wiped out by the cost of an armed convoy to protect coinage, arbitrageurs again and again look for ways to speed up, reduce costs, or otherwise create a differential that will allow them to capture arbitrage profits that previous technologies were too blunt to target.[8] This is precisely the use to which the new communication technologies of the telegraph and telephone were put in the nineteenth century.

Arbitrage and Technology: The Case of "Shunting"

Henry Emery's argument that arbitrage was transformed from an "essential part" of "ordinary trade" into its modern form when it became possible for "prices in both the selling and the buying markets [to be] known at the same moment" is a fascinating claim, coming as it does in a book written at the end of the nineteenth century (1896, 137). By our standards today, telegraph and telephone communication could never be considered instantaneous. Yet Emery highlights a crucial moment in the history of arbitrage when these technologies were introduced. The telegraph, according to James Carey, "permitted for the first time, the effective separation of communication from transportation" (1992, 203). Unlike the previous period when the speed of physical travel limited the speed of the message, the ability to send a message over wires revolutionized communication and "ushered in the modern phase of history" (203). It also allowed a dramatic leap forward in simulated instantaneity and therefore arbitrage.

With the invention of the telegraph in 1838 and the telephone two decades later, the limit point of financial transactions, like that of communication, was breeched. With these technologies, a new form of financial trading known as "shunting," or arbitrage between stock exchanges in different locations, became possible. Shunting occurred when brokers in different cities formed teams between two exchanges, with one buying shares on their home exchange and the other selling short on his; the physical shares of stock were transported for settlement at a later time. The joint-account arbitrage teams, connected via telephone, could trade more quickly and accurately than individual arbitrageurs who relied on the public stock ticker to identify arbitrage opportunities and then cabled orders to brokers on each exchange. What's more, access to telephone wires was available only to brokers who actually owned a seat on a given exchange. Independent brokers who did not own seats on the exchange did not have access to exchange phone lines so they could not hope to perform arbitrage at the same speed as exchange members. Thus, the telephone opened up network differentials between those traders who could access them and those who could not. Finally, arbitrage teams agreed not to charge each other commissions, effectively reducing the cost of trading such that profit was greater (or in some cases became possible at all) than individuals could hope to gain (Weinstein 1931).

Shunting was not limited to domestic markets. Transatlantic shunting occurred regularly but because transatlantic telephone lines were not laid until the mid-twentieth century, it relied on the telegraph. In this case, network differentials were produced by the physical location of privileged arbitrageurs within exchange buildings. An extended quote from Meyer Weinstein's (1931) book, *Arbitrage in Securities*, illustrates the necessary configuration of successful arbitrageurs' networks. Again, an individual arbitrageur phoning or cabling orders to his broker would be at a hopeless disadvantage to the broker located at the "arbitrage rail":

> The New York Stock Exchange had a special arbitrage department on one side of the exchange, which was railed off from the rest of the floor. The arbitrageurs were not permitted to trade on the floor of the exchange, but this was no handicap to their operations. From their position at the rail, they were connected with the offices of the cable companies on the lower floor of the building by pneumatic tubes, through which they sent their cable orders on the other side of the Atlantic. It took them approximately three minutes to complete a transaction of both purchase and sale between the New York Stock Exchange and the London market. (Weinstein 1931, 14)

The fact that communication across the Atlantic could be reduced to mere minutes was a stunning leap forward in speed and connectivity. What previously would have required a boat and at least a week's time was now occurring at almost incomprehensible speeds. In fact, the implications of the telephone and telegraph were so monumental for arbitrage trading that Emery suggested that, by 1896, technology had made arbitrage as nearly instantaneous as could be imagined. In the case of domestic shunting, Emery claimed that trade had reached its apotheosis: "Private wires between the cities, telephones in the exchanges, and operators quick to translate and transmit the signals of the brokers on the floor, constituted an effective machinery for operations of a very interesting kind. By means of these devices the same man was practically trading in Boston and in New York at the same time. A change in price in either place was known by the broker on the floor of the other within less than thirty seconds. This was trade reduced to its finest point" (139).

For Emery, technologically mediated arbitrage was so successful and complete that it had effectively erased price differences between exchanges. Carey, who cites Emery in his discussion of the telegraph, actually claims that prices came to such full parity that the "decline of arbitrage" was one of the most significant outcomes of the introduction of telegraphy (1992, 217). Carey was in some ways correct that the telegraph "[brought] the conditions of supply and demand in all markets to bear on the determination of a price" (217). Stocks on different exchanges would have undoubtedly traded at different prices in the absence of a mechanism to allow discovery of disparities and arbitrage to profit from them. What's more, when the arbitrage Emery describes began to take place, prices did move closer together through supply and demand (Michie 1987). This is the space-annihilating outcome envisioned in the benevolent-efficiency narrative of arbitrage. A single market is achieved as arbitrage overcomes the distances and differences between individual markets.

However, Carey's assertion that this evening out of prices across markets "eliminates opportunities for arbitrage by realizing the classical assumption of perfect information" is a stunning overreach in hindsight (1992, 217). For one, prices between markets can never be equalized once and for all, but must be constantly pushed toward parity through continuous arbitrage operations. Prices fluctuate as speculators and investors buy and sell, and these small fluctuations each offer a new profit opportunity for arbitrageurs if the speed and connectivity of present technologies allow. But, perhaps more importantly, the telegraph was *not* instantaneous. It did not provide "perfect information," but only communication that was faster than the previous speed of transport-communication.

Telegraphy enabled new arbitrage due to this increase in speed. But, as it became more widespread, arbitrage at the speed of the telegraph became easier for others to use, not just the privileged traders who were able to first access it. This increased parity among prices, as more arbitrageurs could jump on momentary disparities and profit from them, but it also made arbitrage more distributed and less profitable since anyone could do it. The diffusion of the technology essentially evened out the network differential.

Elsewhere, I have argued that diffusion of technologies throughout markets results in "increased market coordination" (Hardin and Rottinghaus 2015, 549). This diffusion also "results in dwindling profits and therefore presents a serious problem" for arbitrageurs (549). An arbitrageur who could cut the communication time between exchanges down even further from "less than thirty seconds," that is, construct a more advantageous network differential, stood to profit at the expense of others who still used the old technologies of telegraph and telephone. Far from ending arbitrage, the technological revolution in arbitrage begun by the telegraph touched off a communication technology arms race that is still going on today. It was the first in a long procession of emerging technologies used to create network differentials. Each new technology redefined the possibilities of simulating instantaneity and thus of arbitrage. As John Durham Peters points out in his critique of Carey's utopian claims about arbitrage: "The friction of transporting information may be infinitesimally small compared to transporting cargo, but all kinds of mischief can happen inside of infinitesimally small things" (2006, 148). The history of arbitrage is the history of creating this mischief within more and more infinitesimal time intervals, as arbitrageurs used faster and faster technologies to create new network differentials when old ones evened out.

There is evidence that the New York Stock Exchange (NYSE) was concerned about shunting as early as the 1880s. An 1892 *New York Times* article reports that the exchange was taking "into consideration complaints that have been made of the arbitrage business which is done at the Exchange by brokers having close connections with Boston and Philadelphia."[9] The complaints centered around the fact that brokers who assisted one another with arbitrage on two exchanges did not charge each other commissions but instead "shared the costs incurred, dividing any profits or losses resulting" (Michie 1987, 201). This circumvented the exchange's rules and allowed the arbitrage teams to make larger profits than other traders. The Governing Committee of the NYSE tried several strategies to eradicate the uneven network differential that allowed some arbitrageurs to profit over others. They eventually settled on a "prohibition on sending continuous quotations" from the floor of the exchange via telephone, which effectively curtailed domestic arbitrage by brokers who then had to rely on the slower, riskier, technology of the ticker (201). The exchange thereby banned shunting in 1898. International arbitrage was likewise banned between April 1911 and the beginning of the First World War, as it was believed that "domestic business was being lost overseas" due to the practice (202).

Emery's (and later Carey's) interpretation of shunting as standardizing prices through efficient trading foreshadowed the benevolent-efficiency narrative of arbitrage that would dominate financial economics in the late twentieth and early twenty-first centuries. Yet the practice was so controversial—for both the unfair advantages it exposed and for its negative effects—that both forms of shunting were eventually banned. This would become a pattern in subsequent years each time a new crisis brought arbitrage under public scrutiny.

Putting Arbitrage on a Leash: Index Arbitrage and the "Collar"

After the telegraph and telephone became widespread, other communication technologies were used for the purposes of arbitrage, particularly early computer technologies. In the 1970s and 1980s, developments at the

Chicago Board of Trade (CBOT), Chicago Mercantile Exchange (CME), and NYSE allowed for another dramatic leap in simulating instantaneity. Between 1968 and 1978, the NYSE went from transmitting orders via phone and swapping paper stock certificates at the end of each day to electronic trading and clearance ("Timeline: 1960–1979" 2010). In addition, from 1972 to 1987, the CBOT and CME successfully introduced financial futures on currencies and stock indices, and implemented electronic trading of them as well ("Timeline of CME Achievements" 2015).

Previously, futures were only traded on commodities. Allowing financial futures, and particularly futures on stock indices,[10] created a new kind of arbitrage opportunity. Index arbitrage involves buying (low) a portfolio of stocks that closely approximates an index and entering into a futures contract to sell (high) that index at a future date (or vice versa),[11] on the assumption that when that expiration date arrives, the index and the portfolio will have nearly the same value and the difference between the contracted futures price and the present price will yield a profit. Index arbitrage utilizes futures contracts to stabilize the price of one leg of the deal, the cost of the index at expiry. Through this stabilization, a disparity between the index price today and the index price in the future can be locked in, simulating instantaneity. Assuming that the cost of holding the stocks over the period up to maturity of the futures contract—such as interest on money borrowed for such a purpose—does not erase the difference between today's (spot) price and the futures price, an arbitrage profit can be secured via contract instead of network differentials.

However, the introduction of the Designated Order Turnaround (DOT) system at the NYSE in 1976 and the SuperDOT in 1984, at the same time that financial futures were introduced, led to a high-speed form of index futures arbitrage that yielded enormous profits from small, intermittent fluctuations that were previously too fleeting to capitalize on.[12] Large banks with advanced computer programs were able to engage in automated "program trading": the "coordinated purchase or sale of an entire portfolio of stocks" (Bodie et al. 2009, 66). Program trading relies on computer algorithms, and it therefore allowed index arbitrageurs to trade on small changes in prices for the calculated index and a group of stocks that approximated that index immediately, without a human having to intervene. Programs identified disparities between future and spot prices and automatically sent orders through electronic trading platforms to "almost simultaneously" perform the arbitrage trade (Bodie et al. 2009, 66).

Stock index arbitrage through program trading relies on both kinds of simulated instantaneity: network differentials for those traders with the computer algorithms and access to electronic trading platforms to carry out program trading, and price stabilization through the use of index futures. Automated index arbitrage is only successful for the arbitrageur with the most advantageous network, the one who can develop the best network of computer programs, connections to electronic trading systems, and access to capital to fund the trades. An arbitrageur who sees a disparity and then calls his broker to place an order would find that either the program trading of more sophisticated arbitrageurs had already erased the disparity, or worse, the duration of his slow trade could leave him buying up stocks at spot only to find that he cannot sell a futures contract at a profit. The trade is only successful for the fastest, most well connected, and most capitalized arbitrageur. For the slow arbitrageur, the trade is very risky, as he could be left with a mountain of unhedged stocks.

This example turns the *riskless* term in the financial economic definition of arbitrage on its head.[13] Arbitrage is riskless ex post facto for the arbitrageur who successfully simulates instantaneity at the expense of others. Unlike economists, traders do not assume ex ante risklessness. They are fully aware of the fact that arbitrage can either succeed or fail, as evidenced by this quote from an analysis of program trading: "There is a great deal of competition among arbitragers, arbitragers only place programs when an opportunity exists to execute a program successfully" (Kerr and Maguire 1988, 1004). An economist would say that if the arbitrage was not fully certain from the start, it wouldn't qualify as true arbitrage in the first place. But in reality, since instantaneity can only ever be simulated, the risklessness of arbitrage is contingent on the arbitrageur having the advantage of a network differential and/or price stabilizing contracts. An arbitrageur may only learn that another trader has a better network when he is left holding the bag.

Automated index arbitrage likely began as soon as the SuperDOT system was introduced in 1984. As early as 1985, program trading came under public scrutiny for allegedly producing violent swings in stock prices as large bundles of stocks were bought and sold through the automated system.[14] The criticism of program trading grew after the infamous 1987 stock market crash known as Black Monday. While a great many factors contributed to the 23 percent drop in the Dow Jones Industrial Average that day, commentators eventually blamed the crash on the combination of two different and opposed automated trades, index arbitrage and "portfolio insurance" programs, in the "cascade theory" (Santoni 1988). Portfolio insurance locked in a floor beneath which the value of the portfolio would not fall in the event of a downturn by automating the short selling of futures on indexes that roughly approximated the positions of an investor's portfolio. This generated an excess supply of index futures, however, and index arbitrage, also automated, was designed to trade on a formula that noticed price fluctuations in index futures. The increased supply of futures pushed their prices down relative to spot prices, triggering automated buy orders from index arbitrageurs. To balance the trades, the index arbitrage programs necessarily sold actual stocks short in the present, since they were now trading slightly higher than the futures. This would net a profit when they repurchased the stocks using the futures and returned them to their lenders at expiration.

However, the impact of the index arbitrage activity on the portfolio insurance formula created a positive feedback loop. Arbitrageurs' short-selling of stocks in response to the portfolio insurance trades selling futures meant that the supply of stocks in the present went up, causing prices to fall further. This triggered the portfolio insurers to sell even more futures, thus creating a vicious cycle. Rather than pushing prices back to their correct position, index arbitrage in combination with portfolio insurance artificially depressed prices in a downward spiral that at the very least contributed to the Black Monday crash (MacKenzie 2006).

Despite the complexity of the—at the time very new and technologically advanced—trades that contributed to the crash, a nationwide survey just three weeks after the crash found that 55 percent of those polled said that program trading was a likely cause.[15] After the crash, President Ronald Reagan appointed a special task force known as the Brady Commission to investigate, which published its report in January 1988. Among a number of other recommendations, it suggested that the Federal Reserve devise "some kind of 'circuit breaker' mechanism that would halt trading in certain stock and futures instruments when selling pressure gets too intense."[16] In February 1988, the NYSE took matters into its own hands and restricted program trading, "banning its use for index arbitrage whenever the Dow Jones industrials move up or down 50 points in a day."[17] Under the ban, "On days when the Dow Jones industrial average falls or climbs by more than 50 points, member firms are prohibited from using the exchange's SuperDOT computer system for program trades."[18] This ban, or "collar" as it was called, had the effect of foiling many attempts at arbitrage.[19]

In response, a number of Wall Street firms voluntarily halted index arbitrage altogether, at least on their own accounts.[20] Thus, some index arbitrage was effectively suspended by removing access to the high-speed communication technology (the SuperDOT system) that was a crucial part of simulating instantaneity in the trade. However, not every firm needed the automated system to perform the arbitrage. As it turned out, Goldman Sachs was able to profit more from arbitrage under the ban than it was when everyone had access to the SuperDOT system. Goldman spokesperson Robert Mnuchin explained in 1989 that the collar worked "to the advantage of large firms, such as Goldman, which have enough traders to execute such trades without using the computer system."[21] In other words, due to its size and number of traders, Goldman secured a better network differential with the collar than without. Its human-telephone network dwarfed the networks of other, smaller and less well connected firms, so without the automated technology, Goldman successfully simulated instantaneity better than those firms could without access to the SuperDOT.

When the collar was later removed, Goldman Sachs petitioned the NYSE board to reinstate it, ostensibly for the good of investor confidence, as there was widespread belief that index arbitrage increased market volatility.[22] But, in fact, the SuperDOT technology evened out network differentials among all firms, making markets more efficient and thus reducing opportunities for arbitrage only it could undertake. Goldman's request demonstrates that successful arbitrage doesn't depend on absolute speed but on simulating instantaneity under whatever the given technological conditions. In this case, restricting communal access to the SuperDOT system would have benefited Goldman because it would have reduced market efficiency and allowed the firm to profit from being fastest at using the older, slower telephone ordering system.

Arbitrage at the Speed of Light: High Frequency Trading

Simulating instantaneity requires winning a battle on two fronts: first, against time itself, which threatens to change prices disadvantageously in the time between when a price discrepancy is discovered and when the arbitrage trade is executed. Second, the successful arbitrageur must win against other arbitrageurs whose trading activities may negate or use up the arbitrage profits available from a particular trade. The first battle relates to the dangers of a contingent future unfolding uncertainly. The second relates to the self-negating nature of some (but not all) arbitrage trades over time. The first arbitrageur(s) to carry out a trade may in many cases very quickly exhaust its profitability as the forces of supply and demand bring prices together, leaving slower arbitrageurs out of profit making entirely.

It follows that the ultimate goal of arbitrageurs is to simulate instantaneity, either through network differentials or through price stabilization, better than anyone else. For network differentials, the arms race for the fastest emerging technologies has reached sci-fi proportions. Latency arbitrage, a form of high frequency trading (HFT), utilizes network differentials between high-speed networks and computer algorithms on the one hand, and the slower electronic trading systems of exchanges on the other. A large buy or sell order for a stock will decrease or increase supply and thus increase or decrease price. Latency arbitrage anticipates these changes before the trade actually reaches a central electronic clearinghouse and a new price is calculated and distributed electronically.[23] Arbitrageurs can sell short at the current price knowing that, once the new price is calculated, they can buy the stocks at the new lower price. Latency arbitrage guarantees a profit to those arbitrageurs who are able to, in effect, see the future, to know what the price will be fractions of a second before the price actually changes. Their profit is guaranteed because they trade in the fractions of a second between a price changing event and a change in price, that is, effectively instantaneously.

The network differentials utilized for successful latency arbitrage depend on the speed of communication technologies that give one arbitrageur an advantage over the slower electronic trading systems, but also over other arbitrageurs. If a faster latency arbitrageur buys up all available stock for an anticipated trade before any others, no one else can profit. What's more, the slower arbitrageurs may find themselves entering one leg of the trade only to find the prices changed before they could enter the second. Financial journalist Felix Salmon explains that latency arbitrage is in fact a battle between the fastest arbitrageur who can successfully execute the trade, and the next slowest arbitrageur(s), who fails to do so. Salmon writes: "If you were to actually enter the market with a simple latency-arbitrage algorithm . . . you would almost certainly lose your shirt in no time: a thousand other algobots would immediately recognize your pattern, and pick you off systematically."[24] Therefore, there is a constant push to increase speed to stay ahead of other traders. MacKenzie et al. point out that, in the early 2000s, "high-frequency trading firms rent[ed] space for their computer servers in the same building as an exchange's," a practice known as colocation (MacKenzie et al. 2012, 286). One particular high-frequency trader commissioned a new fiber-optic cable between

Chicago and New York for the purposes of arbitrage, drilling through the Allegheny Mountains to achieve the most direct route. The cable shaved "1.3 milliseconds off the previously fastest one-way time" (287).

As more and more high-frequency traders have used new, faster communication technologies, they have increased liquidity and lowered bid-ask spreads. This diffusion also, however, decreases arbitrage opportunities by evening out previously advantageous network differentials. The result is that many high-frequency traders are now unable to gain a significant advantage. Gregory Meyer, Nicole Bullock, and Joe Rennison explain in the *Financial Times* that "trading firms are struggling to wring profits from the incremental millisecond," and that, between 2009 and 2017, profits to HFT firms fell from $7.2 billion to below $1 billion.[25] Many HFT firms have shut down, and the remaining firms make a fraction of what traditional investment firms make.[26] The result, along with decreasing profits, is a more frantic search for the next fastest method of simulating instantaneity.

This race for new network differentials for latency arbitrage has moved from fiber-optic cables to microwave signals to lasers. In 2014 the engineering firm Anova, in partnership with the military contractor AOptix, completed a laser network connection between exchanges in London and Frankfurt and was set to construct another connecting the NYSE with the NASDAQ to shave *nanoseconds* off the previous connection between the two exchanges for a cost of several billion dollars (Anthony 2014). There is even speculation that SpaceX may be able to provide high-frequency traders with a "satellite-based global internet system" named "Starlink" that could improve speed over microwave transmission (Rosov 2019).

Not everyone believes it is a public service that lowers trading costs and provides more ample liquidity to markets. High-frequency trading has been consistently critiqued for being a form of (illegal) front-running, that is, trading on information before other market participants have it. In 2013 a contributor to CNNMoney claimed that latency arbitrage leaches billions of dollars from "unwitting investors" (Curran 2013). Similarly, the main argument of Michael Lewis's (2014) *Flash Boys* is that HFT is actually front-running.[26] As with shunting and program trading before it, when the mechanics of HFT came to light, many people were outraged that it continues to remain legal.

Falling profits to high-frequency traders do not suggest that latency arbitrage will die off completely, but that there is more competition for the trades, because simulating instantaneity at the expense of other arbitrageurs has become more difficult. To be assured of success, arbitrageurs must hope for new ways to achieve advantageous network differentials. Technologically simulated instantaneity is only ever fleeting. As soon as new technologies are available to many players, previously advantageous network differentials dissolve.

Arbitrage is central to finance, a sought-after form of profit making that traders pay dearly to engage in. As I showed in chapter 2, arbitrage has many defenders who trot out the benevolent-efficiency narrative whenever it is critiqued. But this narrative does not explore the political economic dimensions of arbitrage. Specifically, the question of whether arbitrage is exploitative, which is implicit in some of the denunciations of it recounted in this chapter, has not been explored. In the next chapter, I use Moishe Postone's (1993) critique of Marxism to demonstrate that, while exploitation may seem like a reasonable way to interpret arbitrage, it is better to see it as the goal of a new form of abstract domination that we have yet to fully understand.

FOUR

The Postonian Turn

Mutual funds are investment vehicles in which a number of assets (stocks, bonds, currencies) are pooled together to achieve a diversified and optimized return. Funds may be actively managed or contain a fixed mix of assets, such as an index fund. Individuals can buy shares of the fund instead of having to buy shares of each of the individual assets it contains and manage them on their own. Mutual funds have a long history, but they have grown exponentially in popularity since the 1960s for a number of reasons. First, Joseph Nocera (1994) states that, prior to the 1960s, stock investing was the province of the wealthy. Most people saved using traditional savings accounts that offered a guaranteed and insured if modest return. But in the go-go years of the late 1960s, young, hip mutual fund managers enticed savers to become investors with returns as high as "30 and 40 percent" (48).

Second, the Great Inflation of the late 1970s drove traditional savers from banks to money market and mutual funds. While the return on savings accounts was capped by government regulation—Regulation Q—at between 4 and 6 percent during that period, money market and mutual fund returns were not and usually provided much better return to insulate money from the depreciation effect of double-digit inflation (Nocera 1994, 167, 77). Finally, after the 1978 Revenue Act, there was a profound shift in the United States from traditional pensions that offered a defined retirement benefit provided by employers to defined contribution plans like the

401(k) in which employees invest their own money for retirement, with or without a matching contribution from their employers (Butrica et al. 2007, 3). From 1980 to 2012, the number of private-sector workers whose employers provide a traditional pension plan fell from 38 to 17 percent, while workers participating in defined contribution plans like 401(k)s and IRAS rose in the same period from 8 to 41 percent (Butrica et al. 2007; Bureau of Labor Statistics 2012). As of 2018, 67 percent of 401(k) assets and 47 percent of individual retirement account (IRA) assets were invested in mutual funds (Investment Company Institute 2018). Individual retirement accounts are frequently invested in mutual funds because they purport to offer some guarantee against the risk of individual investing through diversification. However, this diversification is no guarantee of return.

Mutual funds are priced differently from stocks or bonds. Stock prices change continuously and are posted continuously by exchanges during the trading day. In contrast, mutual funds calculate their price or net asset value at the close of trading each day based on the closing prices of component securities (stocks, bonds, etc.). Net asset value (NAV) is calculated by subtracting any liabilities from the total value of all its assets and dividing by the number of shares outstanding (Securities and Exchange Commission 2013).

Mutual fund timing is the practice of buying or selling mutual funds based on stale prices, which allows arbitrageurs to capture a profit from price changes in component assets before they impact the NAV.[1] Todd Houge and Jay Wellman explain how the trading works:

> Market timers utilize information produced during U.S. trading hours that is not fully reflected in daily NAVs. By observing large index movements or trends in similar types of securities, timers are able to predict the direction of future NAV changes. For example, the positive correlation across global financial markets implies that large increases in U.S. equity indexes are often followed by positive changes across international equity markets. Thus, a market timer could purchase international equity funds following a sharp rise in U.S. markets and sell these funds when U.S. markets trend down. This strategy generates significantly positive excess returns because the timer is able to trade at stale net asset values. Moreover, the strategy is perfectly legal. (Houge and Wellman 2005, 132)

Until 4 p.m. EST, the mutual fund's price will still reflect the stale price for the fund. If a savvy investor could see that a component stock will likely have an amazing day, she would buy up many shares of the mutual fund at the lower price, wait until the NAV is recalculated and sell it back the next day for an arbitrage profit.

Mutual fund timing is, like many forms of arbitrage, "theory-dependent" (Beunza, Hardie, and MacKenzie 2006, 733), in that mutual fund timers must employ models to determine the impact that changes to component stocks will likely have on the recalculation of NAV at the end of the day. Any arbitrage trade depends on two things being equivalent, yet having different prices.[2] Arbitrage is also theory-dependent because arbitrageurs often have to convince others, such as managers, that the equivalencies between two securities to be arbitraged are true or risk having to unwind their arbitrage trades before making a profit (733). Thus, what economists describe as a process of discovering price disparities on which to execute arbitrage can actually be seen as more of a creative process. Beunza and Stark argue that arbitrage traders use a number of social and technological tools to "make associations" and "create equivalencies" between securities in order to engage in arbitrage (2004, 380, 382). This is no less the case for mutual fund timing.

Houge and Wellman point out that the practice of mutual fund timing is "perfectly legal," but most mutual funds have policies designed to limit the practice such as "imposing trade limits, initiating short-term redemption fees, and/or actively discouraging rapid trading in the prospectus" since timing can substantially reduce the profits fund investors receive, an effect known as "dilution" (2005, 132, 131). In 2003 New York Attorney General Elliot Spitzer and the SEC investigated several mutual funds for "secretly [allowing] select investors to rapidly trade the portfolio despite statements banning the practice in the prospectus," which basically meant that those privileged investors alone could perform the arbitrage, while regular mutual fund investors could not (132). However, typical investors don't engage in arbitrage anyway; instead, they buy mutual funds for long-term gains. Buy-and-hold investors would also stand to benefit from the increase in NAV the following day insofar as that would be an increase in the value of their long-term investment. However, when mutual funds allow arbitrageurs to buy up lower-priced shares and sell them the following day, the net effect is a smaller increase in the value of the fund for buy-and-hold investors.[3]

This form of arbitrage thus "dilutes" returns for buy-and-hold investors (Houge and Wellman 2005). As Houge and Wellman put it, "the trading profits earned by market timers come at the expense of other long-term investors" (132). Arbitrageurs profit by moving in and out of the fund quickly and skimming off profits those long-term investors are trying to make. In other words, dilution of mutual funds could be understood as a form of exploitation, and a widespread one at that. Before the SEC fined seventeen mutual funds a total of $3.1 billion dollars in 2004 for what amounted to allowing preferred traders to create network differentials through access not granted to all traders (133), research indicates that "relative returns of abused funds were, on average, 4.9 percentage points lower than those of their untainted counterparts each year" (McCabe 2009, 14). Additionally, Eric Zitzewitz estimated in 2003 that, due to mutual fund timing, "long-term shareholders are losing about $5 billion a year across all asset classes" (2003, 246).

Mutual fund timing is therefore a unique case in that, unlike some other forms of arbitrage, the winners and losers are clearly delineated. Arbitrageurs profit at the expense of the mass of everyday investors. As I showed in chapter 3, arbitrage is successful for those traders who can utilize advantages of speed and connectivity in financial networks or those who can stabilize prices artificially through the use of derivatives contracts to simulate instantaneous trading. And the success of those arbitrageurs who best simulate instantaneity to gain a profit always comes at the expense of other market participants who are too slow, disconnected, or unable to stabilize prices to their advantage. In the case of index arbitrage or high-frequency trading, the other market participants are usually other traders attempting arbitrage, not everyday folks investing in mutual funds for retirement.

Mutual fund timing is not done by individual retirement investors, but instead by well-connected hedge funds and other professional traders who have the information technologies to access and act on wide-ranging market information, the financial models to use available information to construct and execute arbitrage opportunities, and depending on the scruples of the mutual fund managers, the differential access to short-term trading to realize profits. In other words, the practice allows one class of traders to very clearly target and negatively impact another entire class of participants. It therefore calls forth a potential critique of arbitrage that mirrors the class-based critique of industrial capitalism offered by Marx.

In *Capital*, Marx explicitly formalizes the relationship of exploitation between workers, whose labor-power produces value, and capitalists, who appropriate a surplus of that value because workers produce more than the value of their own means of subsistence. That is to say, under capitalism, workers produce more than they need to, and rather than delivering the extra value to workers, capitalists pay workers a set wage and appropriate the excess for themselves. Marx calls the ratio of surplus labor to necessary labor the "rate of surplus-value" and states that "the rate of surplus-value is therefore an exact expression of the degree of exploitation of labour-power by capital, or of the labourer by the capitalist" (2003, 209).

The Marxist critique of labor exploitation suggests that the capitalist, in appropriating surplus value, takes something from workers that they rightfully deserve—value—and presents collective ownership of the means of production, in which surplus is also distributed collectively, as the fairer alternative to this dynamic. Visions of socialism or communism usually involve a transition from private ownership of the means of production to collective ownership and "consciously (planned) organized output" (Mandel 1990, 89). As Richard Wolff and Stephen Resnick put it, Marxian theorists' notion of communism includes "collective ownership of all means of production, the allocation of labor power not by market exchange but rather collectively designed economic planning, and the collectively determined disposition of the surplus" (1987, 152–53).

For Moishe Postone, this vision is unique to what he calls "traditional Marxism," which is a set of interpretations in which "relations of domination are understood primarily in terms of class domination and exploitation" because "the surplus product in capitalism is created by labor alone and is appropriated by the capitalist class" (1993, 7, 8). In traditional Marxism, "capitalism is treated as a set of extrinsic factors impinging on the process of production: private ownership and exogenous conditions of valorization of capital with a market economy" and "social domination . . . is class domination, which remains external to the process of production" (9). Postone sees traditional Marxism as "a critique of capitalism from the standpoint of labor" in which the overcoming of capitalism can be achieved by implementing a "new, just, and rationally regulated mode of distribution" (8).

This same interpretation might be applied to the case of dilution. Long-term investors make mutual funds viable. Their investments literally fund the fund. And, since they are funding the fund, they deserve the profits that accrue to it. Arbitrageurs who swoop in and skim off profits with overnight trades are exploiting these investors. They should be prevented from doing so—as the judgments in 2004 ostensibly tried to do—so that a fairer distribution of profits can be achieved (Houge and Wellman 2005).

There are a few immediate problems with this analogy. First of all, Marx's analysis establishes that labor produces value, and he certainly did not suggest that investing does the same. In fact, although they might also be workers who are investing their income for the purpose of saving for retirement, investors are by definition also the selfsame capitalists who do the exploiting in Marx's formalization. Capitalists use their capital to buy the means of production, and the stocks that make up mutual funds are nothing more than shares of the means of production, or if bonds are included, shares of usurious credit. Can mutual fund timing be analogous to capitalist exploitation if it is exploiting the exploiters? Second, viewing mutual fund timing as a form of exploitation suggests that buy-and-hold investing in the absence of arbitrage is something like a fair, socialistic distribution of profits, when buy-and-hold investing is of course only available to those members of society with excess capital to invest. Buy-and-hold investing is no more a fair distribution of wealth in society, in the traditional Marxist sense, than industrial capitalism is. But there is an even more important reason not to take a traditional Marxist view of mutual fund timing as exploitation: the traditional Marxist critique of exploitation is itself flawed, as Postone (1993) convincingly argues. In the next section, I follow Postone's critique of the traditional Marxist understanding of exploitation in order to apply his insights to the case of mutual fund timing and arbitrage in general. Postone's insights provide a necessary pivot from the descriptive analysis of arbitrage I've offered so far to a critical unpacking of the organization of financialized society in which arbitrage plays a crucial role.

Condemned to Labor: Postone's Critique of Marxism

In *Time, Labor, and Social Domination*, Postone critiques traditional Marxism for offering a "transhistorical" and "universal" interpretation that mistakes labor for the source of value in all societies at all times. Instead, Postone sees Marx's immanent description of capitalism as identifying value-producing labor as a unique attribute of capitalism alone: "In Marx's mature critique, the notion that labor constitutes the social world and is the source of all wealth does not refer to society in general, but to capitalist, or modern society alone" (1993, 4). Postone therefore reinterprets Marxism with a different perspective: instead of "a critique of capitalism *from the standpoint of labor*," he offers "a critique *of* labor in capitalism" (5).

Postone shows that Marx's categories of "value, abstract labor, the commodity, and capital" are forms of existence specific to capitalist society, "categories of a critical ethnography of capitalist society undertaken from within" and therefore historically and contextually specific (1993, 18). As he explains, the society in which labor produces value is a unique one: "A society in which the commodity is the general form of the product, and hence value is the general form of wealth, is characterized by a unique form of social interdependence—people do not consume what they produce but produce and exchange commodities in order to acquire other commodities" (148). In this society, labor is not merely a means to an end, but is in fact the process that mediates all social life: "Labor itself constitutes a social mediation in lieu of overt social relations" (150). Rather than overt domination, labor enacts the abstract domination of capitalism in making itself appear necessary for survival, when in fact it is capitalism itself which compels people to labor to survive. In capitalism, supposedly free individuals are "confronted by a social universe of abstract objective constraints that function in a lawlike fashion" (163).

For Postone (1993), the abstract domination of labor is what defines capitalism, and it means that the question of exploitation is not one of the theft of wealth from one group of people by another. Instead, "social domination in capitalism does not, on its most fundamental level, consist in the domination of people by other people, but in the domination of people by abstract social structures that people themselves constitute" (30). In other words, as Geoff Mann explains in his interpretation of Postone, "capitalism is worthy of critique not, principally, because labour does not get enough of the value 'produced'; capitalism is worthy of critique because, in it, labour is condemned to the production of value. Under capital, producing value is what labour must do" (2010b, 175). This is a radical rethinking of the traditional Marxist theory of exploitation in which labor occupies the position of both moral superiority and victimhood. For Postone, and Mann, individuals are condemned to labor in a system of abstract domination that could, and should, be otherwise. It is this Postonian notion of exploitation, or rather of abstract domination as the more central and fundamental problem with capitalism, that must be applied to the case of mutual fund timing to understand its importance as an emblematic case of arbitrage capture.

Geoff Mann's (2010b) work not only clarifies Postone's critique, but also opens the possibility of applying Postone's insights to the case of mutual fund timing. Some Marxist scholars have come close to suggesting that certain forms of financial activity constitute exploitation, but never use that term because true exploitation, that is, surplus value appropriation, can only take place in the productive heart of capitalism.[4] As I explained in chapter 1, for traditional Marxists, the production of fetishized commodities creates value, while the trading of paper claims in the "credit system" is defined as "unproductive labor" using "fictitious capital." Writing after the 2007–9 financial crisis, Mann challenges the notion that value can only be produced by labor, explaining that, while "contemporary capital's power still lies to a significant extent in the expropriation of labour's surplus-product," it is also necessary to reject "the distinction between 'real' and 'fictitious' value," which would suggest that financial securities do not have real value (177, 178). For Mann, value is not defined by being produced by labor, but instead by being equivalent to the money-form within capitalism, and financial securities have become, as much if not more, a privileged store of value within finance, or what Mann calls "a spatially and temporally generalised social relation of equivalence and substitutability under, and specific to, capitalism" (2010b, 180).[5] He therefore rejects the Marxian interpretation that sees labor-produced commodities as the only stores of value and dismisses the idea that financial securities are imaginary or fictitious. Erasing the distinction between the two is a necessary step toward analyzing contemporary capitalism: "The growing power of the rule of value erases, under and for capital, the boundary between finance and the rest of capital, between a financial instrument and a 'real' commodity. The fact of the matter is that, in modern capitalism, the mezzanine-tranche of a CDO and a bushel of wheat are equally subsumed by the rule of value" (186).

Taken together, Mann's injunction to open finance to political economic analysis and Postone's nuanced critique of Marxism suggest that the dilution of mutual fund timing is not exploitation of buy-and-hold investors by arbitrageurs, but an emblematic moment of financial capitalism that demonstrates exactly the social conditions arbitrage requires to function as a form of capture. Mutual fund timing is successful, yielding an arbitrage profit to the traders who engage in it, because investors are compelled to buy mutual funds by a new form of abstract domination that is isomorphic to that of labor. In other words, finance relies on a process that has the same formal function as labor even though its precise content and context are different. For finance, the principle that enacts abstract domination within society and is the condition of possibility of the capture of value is risk.

Condemned to Risk: Two Axioms

The system of abstract domination organized by risk consists, at a minimum, of two particular "objective constraints" (Postone 1993, 163). They are the axiom of risk and return and the axiom of risk measurement. *Axiom* is a term, like capture, that I borrow from Gilles Deleuze and Félix Guattari (2007). They define axioms as "not theoretical propositions, or ideological formulas but operative statements . . . primary statements, which do not derive from or depend upon another statement" (461). In their work, axioms direct flows of value in capitalism. They are statements that operate on value flows to ensure that capitalism can overcome its contradictions and roadblocks. I'm using it in much the same way here, but in conjunction with Postone's notion of abstract domination. These two axioms set up the system of abstract domination in an objective or unproblematic way. They are foundational statements, not common sense themselves, but the building blocks of commonsense notions about how risk operates. And they organize the function of finance and everyday life to direct flows of money to arbitrage capture.

THE AXIOM OF RISK AND RETURN

The axiom of risk and return is a base assumption of all financial economics and of popular contemporary understandings of profit and reward. It is epitomized in the aphorism "no risk, no reward." It captures the notion that reward only comes to those who put something on the line. In finance, it means that the higher the risk of a security, whether measured as variance, beta, or implied volatility, the higher return investors will demand in order to buy that security. For bonds, this means that lower credit ratings indicate higher risk and thus the yield on the bond must be higher to compensate investors for taking on such risk. In the world of everyday borrowing, this means that high interest rates are not just logical, but unquestionable, for higher-risk borrowers. The lower a borrower's credit rating, the higher the interest rate on their loan must be.

The inception of the axiom might be laid at the feet of Frank Knight, who famously declared that profit flows to entrepreneurs who take on uncertainty that cannot "be reduced to an objective, quantitatively determinant probability" (1921, qtd. in Rubenstein 2006, 50). In other words, hedgeable risks can be priced and accounted for, but radical uncertainty is the source of profit. However, during the rise of mathematical finance in the 1950s and 1960s, the relationship between risk and return was enshrined in precisely those "quantitative determinant" probabilities Knight called risk. The Capital Assets Pricing Model (CAPM), which was developed in the mid-1960s and which Donald MacKenzie refers to as "the centerpiece of modern financial economics" (2006, 279), states that the return that can be expected on any stock is equal to the return of the entire market (or representative index such as the S&P 500) multiplied by a risk factor specific to each stock, known as beta. That is, return is proportional to risk.

This axiom is not purely technical. Its logic is at the heart of what Robert Wosnitzer (2014) calls the "speculative ethos" of finance. Wosnitzer explains that, in financial capitalism, "the derivative financial instrument" is, like the commodity in industrial capitalism, the source of "a generative capacity for the production of wealth" (7). Just as the Protestant ethic encapsulated the subjectivity perfected in industrial production, the speculative ethic of proprietary traders drives financial capitalism. Proprietary traders, who act "on behalf of the bank to maximize profit [by] taking what are understood to be speculative bets on a series of risk parameters," embody that speculative ethos best (22). Risk for reward is, for Wosnitzer, "increasingly marking—if not becoming indexical for—the daily routines of everyday life," as the speculative ethos is articulated in and through both finance and the social world (140). A popular finance textbook explains this idea in layman's terms that show the taken-for-grantedness of this axiom: "Naturally, if all else could be held equal, investors would prefer investments with the highest expected return. However, the no-free-lunch rule tells us that all else cannot be held equal. If you want higher expected returns, you will have to pay a price in terms of accepting higher investment risk" (Bodie et al. 2009, 10).

In the case of dilution, the extent to which the axiom of risk and return functions as a full-blown social mediation is clear—the only option to gain return, particularly for retirement, is to submit one's savings to risky investing. This might appear entirely voluntary, as indeed laborers appear to be free, but the changing conditions of capitalism over the last forty years have begun to compel individuals to invest to secure their survival in their later years. Prior to that, the robust welfare state established after the Great Depression, which included the Social Security system, and the convention of traditional pensions for government and some corporate workers, gave some limited guarantee of elder provision for some U.S. citizens.

The attacks on both the welfare state and unions from the 1970s onward, as well as flatlining wages at lower percentiles, have turned retirement income into a profound uncertainty (DeSilver 2018). This uncertainty, and the turn to risky investing to overcome it, have both been part of a conservative political project in the United States that aims to dismantle progressive taxation and public assistance and instead force individuals, or rather nuclear families, to take responsibility for their own uncertain futures through investing. Melinda Cooper (2017) explains: "Neoliberals and libertarians understood the migration from Social Security to individual investment accounts as the most effective way of neutralizing the divide between worker and investor, thereby preempting any possible opposition to neoliberal labor reform. After all, why would worker-investors continue to support public services and progressive income taxes if they too had a stake in the appreciation of financial assets?" (139). In this context, popular cultural discourse has come to fill the void left by material guarantees with a new common sense in the form of financial literacy injunctions to "put your money to work" and invest to produce retirement income. As illustrated by the proliferation of commercials like "The Prudential Walkways Experiment" ("Prudential TV Commercial" 2017), 401(k)s and IRAS have become necessary components of a middle-class American life. In the ad, couples are asked "How much money do you think you'll need in retirement?" The bewildered experiment subjects are exhorted to "choose wisely" as they guess at the number and input it into a terminal in front of a long, plastic-tiled pathway meant to represent years of life after retirement. One couple featured in the commercial enters $513,930. All the couples are then told to walk forward on the pathway to see "how many years that money will last them." They are all shocked and dismayed at how few tiles light up to indicate how short their comfortable retirements will last on their estimated savings. One exclaims "How could this happen?" The commercial then explains the lesson of the exercise: "Let's plan for income that lasts all our years in retirement," that is, start investing with Prudential now, or get left behind ("Prudential TV Commercial" 2017).

Most Americans can't hope to earn even the too small amount of $513,930 through retirement investing. The average balance of an IRA or 401(k) at retirement is around $200,000 (Williams 2016; O'Shea 2019). And that is for the people who are able to invest anything. More than a fifth of Americans have no personal retirement savings. The pressure to invest for retirement is, nevertheless, relentless, with 78 percent of Americans worrying about not having enough.[6] And traditional safe forms of savings are not appropriate, for money stashed under the mattress or placed in a traditional savings account will lose value over time thanks to the inflation target that the Federal Reserve ensures remains between 1 and 3 percent per year (Mann 2010a). Savings held in cash or saved in a CD yielding 0.75 percent shrinks over time because of inflation. By contrast, popular finance commentators never tire of proclaiming the long-term average of stock returns to be around 7 percent (Pomroy 2016). Under these circumstances, risking your money by investing for retirement rather than "just saving" is the safest, most rational, most necessary way to ensure retirement income in the future. In other words, just like labor, "the compulsion exerted is impersonal and 'objective,' it seems not to be social at all but 'natural.' . . . This structure is such that one's own needs, rather than the threat of force or other social sanctions, appear to be the source of such necessity" (Postone 1993, 161). Therefore, one may easily revise Postone's concise statement "One must labor to survive" (161), as "One must invest to survive," with the weighty caveat that this activity is not available to many living under financial capitalism, for whom the erosion of the welfare state is not an injunction to invest, but a direct immiseration.[7]

That this axiom of risk and return facilitates a system of abstract domination that promotes arbitrage capture follows directly from the fact that things could be otherwise, and indeed have been otherwise. Social Security and traditional pensions were born out of the belief that citizens deserve a baseline standard of living in old age and that compensation in retirement is a reward for years of a job well done. The idea that the only way to secure future income necessary for a decent life after retirement is to risk what money one has in securities trading is just as bizarre and constructed a state of affairs as individuals not consuming what they produce, but rather producing to earn a wage to purchase what they need to consume.

Risky investing is thus, in the case of mutual fund timing, compelled by the axiom of risk and return. It is also, as I have already shown, the very basis for arbitrage that results in the capture of profits by arbitrageurs and the dilution of returns to buy-and-hold investors. Therefore, mutual fund timing and dilution should not be critiqued from the standpoint of the investor, but, as Postone suggests, investing itself is worthy of critique. Or, rather, any critique of financial capitalism must ask why and how we have been condemned to risk by investing in financial markets. For Paul Langley (2008), "everyday investment" entails retirement investing with 401(k)s and IRAs, but also individual investing through online and discount brokers and day trading. We could reasonably add to this list investing for college through federal 529 plans and real estate investing. Popular cultural phenomena like the bestseller *Rich Dad, Poor Dad* (Kiyosaki and Lechter 1998), an overabundance of financial advice and self-help from figures like

Suze Orman, and government-sponsored financial literacy curricula all suggest that investing is a rational and necessary way to provision oneself in the era of reduced social insurance and unconventional (i.e., precarious) work. Each of these practices also puts investors in the path of more sophisticated arbitrageurs who can skim profits off of their investments. But investing for retirement is not the only case in which risk constitutes a form of abstract domination that enables arbitrage capture. Both forms of what Paul Langley (2008) calls "everyday finance"—investment and borrowing—are organized by capture-enabling risk within contemporary financial capitalism. Risky borrowing is more fundamentally wedded to a second axiom, that of risk measurement.

THE AXIOM OF RISK MEASUREMENT

The axiom of risk measurement is, in some ways, more fundamental than the axiom of risk and return, as it concerns the question of how risk can be measured. Standard financial discourse, and nearly all critical treatments of finance, frame risk as a naturally occurring phenomenon that can be measured in various ways (Hardin and Rottinghaus 2020). Yet, at the most fundamental level, risk is not an observable variable, but rather is a characteristic of the unfolding of an uncertain future. Risk is the potential deviation from an expected outcome. But since any expected outcome is necessarily in the future, and therefore uncertain, risk attempts to predict the full spectrum of future events, and the probability of each. For processes governed by more or less accepted natural laws, like the rising and setting of the sun, risk calculation seems unnecessary. For things that follow more complex but still relatively rigid rules, like weather, risk calculation seems important, but imprecise at best. For things like human behavior, that follow highly complex, changeable, and changing rules (if they follow any at all), risk calculation appears downright quixotic. Yet it is this latter context to which financial risk measurement directs itself.

The notion that financial risk is measurable is fundamentally necessary to financial activity and a taken-for-granted primary principle of financial economics. The notion that uncertain outcomes could be predicted using probability dates back at least to the eighteenth century if not before (Bernstein 1998). Yet the probabilities that Frank Knight (1921) distinguished from uncertainty under the name *risk* were not the risk measurements of today. In John von Neumann and Oskar Morgenstern's (1944) game theory, risk was a subjective attitude, not a measurable variable. Harry Markowitz substituted historical variance for risk in his optimal portfolio formula, implicitly suggesting that future deviations from expected returns would mirror those that occurred in the past (Rubenstein 2006). In 1973 the Black-Scholes-Merton options pricing formula went furthest in objectifying risk, when risk became an output of, rather than an input to, the formula. The "implied volatility" term that the formula produces purports to capture the present volatility of a stock (Latané and Rendleman 1976). In other words, it appears to give the present risk of a stock, a seemingly objective measure of the instantaneous potential deviation of a stock from its expected price.

However, financial models cannot actually predict future states of the world, as the history of financial markets has demonstrated time and again. Nassim Taleb (2007) has described those events so wildly outside of financial models' predictions as Black Swans. Financial economists speak of "fat tails" as a way to account for events that are practically impossible in normal pricing models (Fox 2009, 33). The stock market crash on Black Monday in 1987 is one such event. Economists like to point out that it was a "20 sigma event," meaning that its probability lies twenty standard deviations away from the center of the price distribution (Chandrashekaran 1998, 3). Typical financial models predict a crash of that magnitude would occur less than once in the history of existence.

Everyday borrowing depends entirely on this axiom through credit scoring and risk-based pricing, which assigns higher interest rates to supposedly riskier borrowers. Consumer credit—the name analysts give to all those forms of borrowing that allow individuals to procure the trappings of American life without up-front capital—is as old as the republic (Calder 1999). Nineteenth-century retailers kept a book where customers' debts for everyday expenses were logged, but interest was not charged and book credit was not a profitable practice. When individuals needed cash—often due to a misfortune like illness or job loss—they turned to loan sharks who charged interest in excess of 100 percent per year. Consumer lending with interest was formalized as a legitimate business in the 1920s. In the century since, credit in all forms—from mortgage loans and car loans, to student loans and durable goods loans for things like appliances and furniture—has been a central feature of American consumer culture. Contemporary credit cards that offer revolving balances entered the scene in the 1950s, and grew in both profitability and cultural importance in the 1980s and 1990s (Hyman 2011). Today, consumer credit in all of these forms is ubiquitous.

The compulsion to borrow derives in part from the American ideological commitment to consumption, which brings with it the typically American consumer excess of buying things that are used quickly and thrown out or placed in ministorage when they overwhelm comparatively enormous houses. But there are also social consequences for nonparticipation, what Juliet Schor (1998) refers to as "social alienation." Noncompliance with consumer culture has real social and interpersonal consequences like exclusion and violating norms that continuously police Americans into compliance. Consumer culture in the United States is not a personal choice to favor extravagant desires over base needs, but a complex system of advertising, social comparison, and aspirational American Dreamism that produces a compulsion not just to always consume, but to always consume *more*.

This compulsion affects more than just the middle class and upper classes who have, to varying degrees, income and wealth to spend on consumption. It enforces itself on people of all income levels, compelling the use of credit to meet the demands of consumption. Debt doesn't just allow low-income individuals to consume up to the standard of the middle class, but instead is used by people at every income level to consume more than their income allows, even at the highest levels (Schor 1998). More than a third of the top 10 percent of earners carry credit card debt ("Survey of Consumer Finances" 2016). Schor (1998) explains this relative aspirationalism as a compulsion to consume at a level just above that allowed by one's income.

What's more, the contemporary competitive consumption phenomenon emerged around the same time that actual incomes leveled off after the postwar boom. Since the 1970s, wages for the lowest-earning workers have been effectively flat and wages for middle earners have only increased modestly, while incomes of the top 10 percent have seen the greatest increases (DeSilver 2018). That is, the compulsion to spend more all the time has coincided with the inability to do so through wage gains, leading to a double whammy of consumer desire and inability to earn enough to consume. The story is exacerbated by the increase (in real terms) in the costs of homeownership, rent, higher education, healthcare, and childcare ("Consumer Price Indexes"). The cost of everyday life continues to climb while wages lag. Since the 1970s, and particularly since the Supreme Court *Marquette* decision of 1978 that effectively ended state usury laws, debt has rushed in to fill the gap (Manning 2000).

However, specifically mortgage borrowing hasn't been just about the mismatch of means and desires; it has also been the object of political intervention. Since the New Deal, the U.S. government has a long history of promoting homeownership by pumping capital into the secondary mortgage market, first for middle-class suburban borrowers, and later for low-income minorities. The Federal Housing Authority specifically worked to facilitate mortgage-funded homeownership by standardizing and subsidizing the buying process, while the government-sponsored enterprises (Fannie Mae, Freddie Mac, etc.) made sure capital was always available for mortgage lending. In the 1990s, both Bill Clinton and George Bush pushed homeownership as a form of "asset-based welfare" that would supposedly improve the economic station of the poor and minorities without government welfare (Cooper 2017). Fiona Allon and Guy Redden (2012) explain that "government initiatives to expand homeownership opportunities repeatedly reinforced this message of the home as 'asset.' In effect, the homeowner was called upon to be a 'citizen-speculator' and embrace financial market risk" (381).

Culturally, mortgage-funded homeownership has come to occupy a special place in U.S. consumer society. Specifically, "housing speculation has become an elaborate cultural-economic practice that invests the home with profound promise to enhance life" (Allon and Redden 2012, 382). What was once a place to live became both a way to demonstrate wealth and an investment to help you accumulate wealth: "The meanings of both housing and home ownership have been fundamentally recalculated: rather than being seen as a social right or basic need, or as a way of demonstrating national belonging, they have been recast in explicitly financial terms as investment vehicles, as a means of accumulating wealth, and as objects of financial speculation" (Allon and Redden 2012, 380). Allon and Redden see the genre of makeover television shows on networks like HGTV as emblems of the dual role that the home plays in American life: "The overarching imperative of makeover narratives is the production of subjects who can not only generate value for themselves, for their own edification, but also signify their value to others in the social contexts of their lives" (386).

The axiom of risk measurement has facilitated the change and expansion in mortgage and other forms of consumer borrowing. Before the 1960s, debt was available only to those people who underwriters felt would likely honor their repayment obligations (Hyman 2011). The first computerized credit bureau was established in 1965, but underwriting was still largely subjective and discriminatory, meaning that middle-class and wealthy white males made up the vast majority of borrowers (Langley 2008). After the passage of the Fair Credit Reporting Act and Equal Credit Opportunity Act, it became illegal to discriminate against borrowers of particular genders or races. Banks that were now forbidden from using discriminatory underwriting processes turned to supposedly objective algorithms meant to determine the riskiness of the borrower. The underwriting decision could thus be made on the basis of an objective risk measurement rather than categories like race or gender.

The *Marquette* decision came directly on the heels of these changes, and it released banks from usury ceilings that held down the interest rates they could charge on credit cards and other forms of consumer credit. At the time, the decision saved banks from the crush of stagflation, which made lending at capped interest rates unprofitable (Nocera 1994). But it also quickly ushered in a seismic shift in consumer credit to "risk-based pricing" (Langley 2008, 150). Banks could now calculate the risk of a borrower and instead of using it to decide whether or not to lend, they used it to determine the interest rate a borrower should receive on her credit. Low-risk borrowers, who were sure to pay back their mortgage or credit card bill according to their credit profile, could pay low rates of interest since banks were certain they would get their money back. But high-risk borrowers, in risk-based pricing, are not totally shut out from borrowing. Instead, they get subprime or relatively higher rates of interest, based on the logic encapsulated in the axiom of risk and return. The logic goes that, since lenders are unsure whether risky borrowers will fully pay back a loan, they want to collect as much as possible as quickly as possible up front to compensate for the possibility of default. Banks are going out on a limb, so they deserve to get paid more.

What was once a market with low, standard interest rates on credit offered to a limited segment of society became a much broader, but also more stratified one. Computerized credit scoring offered a way to "democratize" credit by removing human judgment from credit decisions (Lauer 2017, 234). But once combined with stratified interest rates, credit democratization began to look less like a way to expand the middle-class standard of living and reduce inequality in the realm of personal finance, and more like a new and different form of "credit inequality" (Manning 2000, 131).

The axiom of risk measurement drives risk-based pricing. As Donncha Marron (2007) explains, "From the 1970s, a technocratic, statistical expertise gradually became applied by lenders to the problem of regulating default within populations of borrowers" (105). The extension of credit became organized around a naturalized notion of "'objective' risk," calculated with statistical models by credit bureaus and banks (105). In particular, "credit scoring was encoded in 'Regulation B' of the [Equal Credit

Opportunity Act of 1974], explicitly delineating what could constitute a statistical model by defining it as one based on the analysis of key applicant attributes and default based on statistically representative sample groups. . . . The act effectively gave legislative recognition to scoring systems as being objective, scientific devices permitting a dispassionate, empirically derived account of creditworthiness and explicitly identified the role they could play in eliminating 'subjective' discrimination" (110).

Today, credit surveillance has expanded to incorporate numerous data points including such seemingly unrelated activity as social media posts (Madden et al. 2017). Additionally, credit reports are routinely accessed not only by institutional lenders but also by potential employers and landlords (Madden et al. 2017). Unsurprisingly, through risk-based pricing, objective credit scoring reproduces the very systematic inequalities in American society—along the lines not only of class but also of race, gender, and even location—that it was supposed to erase (Hyman 2011; Madden et al. 2017). The poor and disadvantaged pay more, while the well-to-do pay less. Risk-based pricing makes long-standing moral judgments about wealth and class into statistical, objective, and seemingly natural facts. Far from ending discrimination, computerized credit surveillance combined with risk-based pricing makes structural inequalities even more unassailable.

Borrowing today requires that individuals submit themselves to the process of risk measurement, the results of which may in very real ways determine their fate. A poor credit score will mean higher interest rates— and thus more difficulty in paying back debt. It may also mean loss of job opportunities and the inability to secure transportation and housing. The system no longer targets particular people specifically for their identities, but instead disadvantages them based on the abstract principle of risk. And, just like investment, borrowing provides a basis for arbitrage capture, through the financial circuits that connect it to risky investing. These circuits are made possible by the technique of financial securitization.

Langley (2008) notes that securitization of various forms of consumer credit—from mortgages and credit card balances, to car loans and student loans—connects everyday borrowing practices to financial markets by bundling debt and selling it to investors as bond-like instruments. In securitization, banks pool debt and sell it to investors to recoup the capital lent immediately, rather than waiting for repayment over time. Investors are the ones who then receive debt payments, not the original lenders. Securitization offers multiple opportunities for arbitrage, as I explain in detail in chapter 5. The main mechanism, however, is relatively simple. Interest payments to debt may be passed through from borrowers directly to investors in the process of securitization, or, as was the case in many of the mortgage securitization deals undertaken in the years leading up to the financial crisis, some of those interest payments can be appropriated by securitizers. In this case, securitizers perform an arbitrage trade. The risk-based pricing that took hold in consumer credit markets in the 1980s makes this arbitrage much more likely and much more profitable. Borrowers who would have previously been denied credit due to their risk profiles are instead offered it, but with relatively high rates of interest. These high rates of interest increase the potential spread between the income and the outlay of securitizations, that is, the excess available for capture. All securitizers must do is find a way to sell the securities for less than the income paid on the loans that underlie them, which is just what securitizers of subprime-backed collateralized debt obligations did before the crisis. The riskier the underlying loans, the larger that spread may be. The larger the spread, the greater the arbitrage.

Most important, this arbitrage is only possible if the mass of everyday consumers put their money at risk through investing and borrowing on a continuous basis. As Miranda Joseph (2014) argues, "The ideal entrepreneurial subject of neoliberalism . . . borrows and invests to build a future for herself and her family" (62). But also, this is a subject "likely to be inhabited in the mode of failure" (62) Joseph shows that this subjectivity is rife with contradiction, as she is enjoined to take responsibility by engaging in the risky activities of investing and borrowing. One of the contradictions that Joseph gestures toward is that, when the subject of neoliberalism puts herself at risk, the rewards flow not to her, but to the arbitrageurs for whom her risk is the raw material of capture.

For Fiona Allon (2010), under conditions of financialization, "risk . . . becomes a way of life, requiring the individual to develop, in the words of the financial planners, a healthy appetite for risk, something that must be grasped and managed in order to maximize returns and rewards in social practices that are now framed as investment decisions" (374). This form of subjectivity isn't really a choice, as "there really did seem to be little alternative to jumping on board and becoming an investor in the ownership society, the shareholder nation, the property-owning democracy" (379). Instead, the imperative to risk is a two-sided system of abstract domination, constructed as the necessity to invest and borrow, that has lifted arbitrage to its central position in financialized capitalism.

FIVE

Money Machines

In 2020 in New York City, the combined federal, state, and city taxes on a pack of cigarettes was \$6.85. But many New Yorkers pay less in cigarette taxes than the official rate. That's because cigarette smugglers import their wares from states where the taxes are far lower, like New Hampshire and Virginia (Bishop-Henchman and Drenkard 2014). This is an arbitrage trade. Smugglers buy the cigarettes—sometimes by the truckload—where they are cheap, and transport them into the city where they are expensive to sell them. It's also an example of what I call money machine arbitrage. Unlike algorithmic stock trading that identifies small price discrepancies and, by arbitraging them, pushes prices together through the mechanism of supply and demand, cigarette smuggling does nothing to remediate the difference in the prices of cigarettes between states. Instead, it costs state governments \$5 billion a year in lost tax revenue.[1] That's because the high price of cigarettes in New York City is the result of policy—in this case taxes—that has become a structural feature of the cigarette market rather than an accidental fluctuation in price. The price discrepancy in the cigarette market is long-lasting, meaning that arbitrageurs can continually trade on it for profit without the risk of negating the discrepancy. The cigarette price discrepancy is like a door propped open, one that money continually flows out of. Cigarette arbitrage is a money machine.

Money machines are exceptional in two ways. First, they are an exception to dominant definitions of arbitrage in which supply and demand make the price discrepancies that arbitrage exploits self-negating. But, second, they are also exceptional in the sense of being the most effective, and therefore most sought-after and preferred, form of arbitrage profit making. Arbitrage that quickly dissolves under the pressure of trading generates fleeting profit. High-frequency traders must trade with such high frequency in order to multiply the fleeting and small profits available to them. Money machines generate continuous profit. That is why the arbitrage in subprime securities—a money machine trade—that began in the late 1990s and accelerated until the credit crunch of 2007 was so attractive to banks and hedge funds who piled into it with enthusiasm.

In this chapter, I first explore the self-negating nature of arbitrage in more detail, in order to show just how thoroughly money machine arbitrage contradicts the benevolent-efficiency narrative that arbitrage makes market prices fair. Second, I describe the subprime CDO money machine trade that preceded the financial crisis. Last, I detail the structural conditions that allowed financial firms to perform "alchemy" on mortgage-backed securities so as to continuously generate profit (Benmelech and Dlugosz 2009).

Self-Negating Arbitrage

Arbitrage is, according to economic theory, a self-limiting trading process.[2] Buying a security where it is priced low, and selling it where it is priced high should—if market participants are rational and markets are efficient—result in the two prices converging through the dynamic of supply and demand. The arbitrageur's activities increase demand for the low-priced security, thus increasing its price; and they increase supply for the high-priced security, decreasing its price (see figures 5.1 and 5.2). When their prices reach parity, either because they become equal or because no additional profit could be made on the trade due to transaction costs (such as brokerage fees or transportation costs), the arbitrage has negated itself. It no longer produces profit and so is no longer undertaken by arbitrageurs.

The economic assumption that arbitrage operates this way is often explained through futures arbitrage. Futures are contracts to buy or sell something at an agreed-upon future date. Futures' prices should adhere to a parity formula with current (spot) prices, where the futures price is equal to the cost of borrowing enough money to buy the security in question today and hold it until the expiration date of the futures contract. The idea is that both of these things would result in the same outcome. If you enter

Arbitrage Opportunity

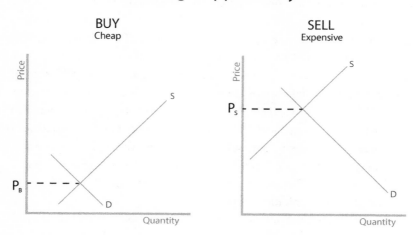

Convergence

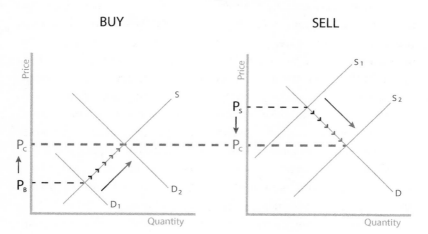

FIGURES 5.1 AND 5.2 The Law of One Price is theoretically ensured by the actions of arbitrageurs and the dynamics of supply and demand. As arbitrageurs buy the cheap good, they increase demand ($D_1 \rightarrow D_2$). As they sell the expensive good, they increase supply ($S_1 \rightarrow S_2$). Prices thereby converge to P_C.

the futures contract to buy one share of Apple stock on October 10, or if you borrow the money necessary to buy one share today and just pay the interest on that sum until October 10, you'll have one share of Apple stock on October 10 in either case. Therefore, the price of the futures contract must equal the cost to borrow and buy that share today.

This example also explains the self-negating feature of arbitrage. If futures prices are higher than the cost to borrow and buy at spot, traders will stop buying futures; instead, they will *sell* futures (after borrowing and buying the underlying stock), knowing that they can make a profit from the difference between the cost of the stock and the high futures price. But this will increase the supply of futures. It will also increase demand for shares of Apple. Futures prices will therefore fall, and Apple prices will rise, meeting in the middle at parity.

Futures prices more or less adhere to the spot-future parity rule, subject to several additional conditions that are all explained in finance textbooks and whose influence is incorporated into the formula.[3] Donald MacKenzie (2006) examined the way that options prices adhere to their own parity formula after the Black-Scholes-Merton formula was published in 1973. MacKenzie argues that the adherence is a form of performativity, where markets performed into reality the relationship the economic formula said should exist. Like futures pricing, the option put-call parity formula relies on arbitrage and the mechanism of supply and demand to bring the prices of call options and put options into parity (Hull 2009, 208). In other words, the idea that arbitrage moves prices into parity through supply and demand is settled law in economic theory. While exceptions exist in real-life trading, they are conceptualized as limits that do not challenge the rule.

Arbitrage trades that do not eventually lead to price parity would be regarded as exceptional, suboptimal errors that should be corrected by allowing markets to be free and open so that supply and demand can produce arbitrage's self-regulatory "discipline" (Roye 2001). However, there is reason to challenge the framing of exceptions to the self-negating rule of arbitrage as limits, since economic notions of arbitrage serve to justify and enable arbitrage capture. Instead, arbitrage that is not self-negating is a counterexample to the misleading and dubious benevolent-efficiency narrative of arbitrage that frames it as a public service, and arbitrageurs as friendly police officers who assure the parity of prices that make markets efficient. Money machines that yield continuous profits instead of negating themselves perform no market discipline at all. They are also the best-case scenario and ultimate goal of professional proprietary traders. Far from being the benevolent police of free and open markets, traders are—much more than many subjects to which the label is applied—profit-maximizing agents who, according to both logic and evidence, prefer the most profit possible. Arbitrageurs therefore strive not for the idealized self-negating arbitrage, but the money machine. What's more, when money machines are found or, more accurately, deliberately created, arbitrageurs excitedly pursue them.

In her book, *Something for Nothing: Arbitrage and Ethics on Wall Street,* finance professor Maureen O'Hara chronicles several money machines, which she labels as "unethical" arbitrage trades (2016, 49). One example involves Goldman Sachs's ownership of an aluminum storage company, Metro International Trade Services. Regulators required that Metro move a minimum amount of aluminum out of its storage facility if there was a queue of requests to exit. However, Metro didn't have to move more than that minimum no matter how long the queue. So, if the queue was very long, it could move small amounts of aluminum every day and charge rent to the owners who were waiting to move their aluminum out while they waited. Goldman incentivized some owners to enter the queue with rebates in order to inflate the queue and receive more rent from owners who actually wanted to move their aluminum out (O'Hara 2016).

When Goldman bought Metro in 2010, the queue was 40 days long. In 2014 it had risen to 674 days, significantly increasing rental income. For O'Hara, Goldman's actions were unethical because "the delays in the aluminum market were not the result of normal commercial behavior, but stemmed from an explicit decision to exploit the storage queue rules" (2016, 124). However, they were legal because "Goldman adhered to the letter of the LME rules" (123). Most importantly, the profits to the trade did not decrease the more that Goldman incentivized owners to enter the queue, but increased, as it was a money machine trade. Like cigarette smuggling, the profit came specifically from exploiting structural conditions, in this case the minimum that made the price of incentivizing owners to enter the queue less than the resultant rental income that could be made by only moving the minimum amount of aluminum each day.

O'Hara also recounts the energy trading strategy undertaken by JP Morgan Chase (and referenced in the introduction of this book) and again claims it is an unethical exception to the rule that "arbitrage removes inefficiencies" (2016, 26). However, I would argue that these are not exceptions; hugely powerful banks did not make occasional wrong turns into unethical practices while pursuing their ultimate goal of benevolently policing unfair market conditions. Instead, they specifically sought out money machines because they provide continuous rather than limited profits. While both Goldman Sachs's and JP Morgan Chase's activities spurred regulators to change rules in their respective markets, the pursuit of money machines goes on. In the next section, I lay out in detail the money machine trade in subprime mortgage backed securities that occurred in the run-up to the financial crisis. I demonstrate that, far from policing unfair prices, the trade relied on financial alchemy that allowed exactly the same securities to trade at different prices, with the blessing of regulators, traders, and other market participants.

The Subprime Money Machine

The Financial Crisis Inquiry Commission (FCIC) was created by an act of Congress in 2009 to examine the causes of the global financial crisis (United States 2011). Its 662-page report, published in 2011, is a comprehensive description of the historical conditions that led up to the crisis and the way it unfolded. The report also contains an entire chapter dedicated to what the authors call "The CDO Machine" (129). The machine language is fitting, as they write that "the CDO became the engine that powered the mortgage supply chain" (129). I agree with this characterization but with the caveat that, whereas the FCIC authors describe the profits from the creation of collateralized debt obligations (CDOs) as fees, I argue that the CDO machine was actually a money machine producing continuous arbitrage profits on the order of billions of dollars in the early 2000s.

The CDO machine required subprime mortgages as a raw material or input. The designation *subprime* refers to the relative riskiness of those borrowers who, according to the logic of risk-based pricing, must pay higher interest rates on their mortgages (Langley 2008). Risk-based pricing works on the logic of the axioms of risk and return and risk measurement. It assumes that the risk a borrower will default can be encapsulated in a single score, which is taken as an objective criterion, and then that this score justifies such borrowers receiving higher rates of interest to compensate for the potential loss a lender opens itself to by issuing them a loan. The history of mortgage lending reveals that, for most of the twentieth century, banks had a relatively low ceiling on the risk they were willing to take on in mortgage loans. People who were poor credit risks simply didn't get mortgages. Part of the reason for this was that, up until 1980, interest rates were capped for first mortgages (Gramlich 2007, 16). Importantly, Wall Street was the main catalyst for issuing high-interest loans to risky borrowers. In this section, I give a brief history of subprime mortgages and mortgage-backed securities in order to explain exactly how they became the raw material for CDO arbitrage.

A BRIEF HISTORY OF MORTGAGE FINANCE

The modern mortgage is a product of post-Depression politics. Prior to the Great Depression, mortgages were short term—one to five years—and required large bullet payments of the entire principal of the loan at maturity (Green and Wachter 2005; Hyman 2011, 48). Conventionally, mortgage holders would refinance their loans at maturity if the lump sum payment was too large to make all at once. After the stock market crash of 1929 and the ensuing Great Depression, banks refused to refinance these short-term loans when they came due, and strapped mortgage holders couldn't pay them off. Almost 10 percent of mortgages went into foreclosure, worsening the depression (Green and Wachter 2005, 95).

The thirty-year, fixed-rate mortgage was created—through a long process that culminated in 1948—as a way to forestall future crises and avoid "socialization of the housing industry" (Zimmerman, qtd. in Hyman 2011, 53).[4] During the Great Depression, the possibility of federally funded affordable housing was seriously considered, but was scrapped in favor of a system for facilitating a secondary market in mortgages. First, as part of the New Deal, the Federal Housing Administration (FHA) was created in 1934. The FHA issued guidelines for construction of new homes and insured mortgages issued on homes that conformed to those guidelines. The purpose of that insurance was to attract investors to the secondary market in mortgage loans to increase mortgage lending. Federal Housing Administration guidelines would assure potential investors that the mortgages were sound (Hyman 2011).

Longer terms, amortization—equalization of payments over the life of the loan—and FHA insurance helped convince investors that the loans could and would be paid back. The Federal National Mortgage Association (Fannie Mae) was created in 1938 to serve as a middleman, trading mortgages between lenders and investors, pumping new capital into mortgage lending. Before the FHA, there was some mortgage resale, but it was not a guaranteed or liquid market. After the standardization of homes through FHA guidelines and the implementation of mortgage insurance, investing in secondhand mortgages offered a low but federally guaranteed profit, and mortgage lending exploded (Hyman 2011). As economists Richard Green and Susan Wachter put it, "America was transformed from a nation of urban renters to suburban homeowners: the ownership rate among U.S. households rose from 43.6 percent in 1940, the last census year before World War II, to 64 percent by 1980" (2005, 97).

However, this change was mostly limited to the white suburbs that allowed for the space and location requirements outlined in the FHA *Underwriting Manual*. The manual gave preferential treatment to homogeneous neighborhoods and explicitly redlined (refused to insure homes in) Black neighborhoods (Hyman 2011). Even after the FHA changed its practices, "finding buyers for [Black] mortgages" on the secondary market was difficult because secondary market buyers were usually "large white-controlled insurance companies" (142). Black insurance companies, like Mutual Life Insurance Company in Durham, North Carolina, bought some FHA mortgages, but they remained largely a perk for the white middle class.

Fannie Mae promoted the secondary market for mortgages by buying whole loans from small banks and lenders and selling them to large institutions. However, uninsured mortgages were still the majority and banks and savings and loans were still the main lenders. In 1968, in response to a tightening of conventional mortgage markets as depositors transferred their money into higher yield Treasury bills, Fannie Mae was split into the Government National Mortgage Association (Ginnie Mae) and the new Fannie Mae (Green and Wachter 2005). The former was tasked with administering the FHA insurance program. Fannie Mae was privatized, but retained a government charter and mission to stabilize and invigorate mortgage markets by buying non-government-backed conventional mortgages, that is, mortgages that adhere to certain guidelines but are not federally insured. Shortly thereafter, the Federal Home Loan Mortgage Corporation (Freddie Mac) was created in 1970 to do the very same thing, but buying specifically from savings and loans rather than mortgage companies (Green and Wachter 2005; Hyman 2011). This new fuller slate of "government sponsored enterprises" (GSEs) went about funding the secondary market for mortgages in a wholly new way, by selling mortgage-backed securities (MBS). Unlike whole loans, mortgage-backed securities gave investors certificates representing diversified pools of loans.

Beginning in 1970, Ginnie Mae lent its government guarantee to mortgage "pass-through" securities, which allowed investors to purchase a bundle of FHA and/or VA loans from mortgage companies (Hyman 2011, 228).

These securities delivered the principal and interest payments to investors, minus only modest fees. With Ginnie Mae's guarantee, defaults would never impact investors, so the securities were attractive.[5] Fannie Mae and Freddie Mac, which already purchased and resold mortgages, quickly began issuing MBS themselves. Their securities were also guaranteed, but since they are private corporations, that guarantee was not backed "by the full faith and credit of the U.S. government."[6] That small detail didn't deter investors, who craved access to the robust profits of mortgage lending without having to get into the business themselves. Mortgage-backed securities were also attractive because they offered inbuilt diversification in the pooling of many mortgages. Purchasing whole mortgages meant that any default would have to be fully absorbed. Buying a pool of mortgages "brought enough diversification, it was believed, to overwhelm any outlying bad loan" (231). Mortgage securitization grew rapidly and transformed the mortgage market from one dominated by large institutions like insurance companies into a fully financialized, capital market–funded enterprise. Hyman explains that, only three years after securitization began in 1973, "FNMA [Fannie Mae] was, next to the Treasury, the largest debt-issuing institution of U.S. capital markets" (232).

The arbitrage in subprime securities that occurred in the run-up to the 2007 financial crisis relied on three interrelated changes in the market for MBS in the 1980s and 1990s: (1) the increase in subprime mortgage lending, (2) the initiation of private label securitization, and (3) the invention of structured finance or securitizations with multiple tranches. First, subprime lending began after the Depository Institutions Deregulatory and Monetary Control Act of 1980 "effectively abolished usury laws on first-lien mortgages" (Gramlich 2007, 16). Mortgage companies took advantage of the new state of affairs to offer higher interest rate mortgages to riskier borrowers. These loans did not conform to FHA standards, but they were potentially highly lucrative due to their high interest rates. Mortgage companies could not sell these loans to Fannie Mae and Freddie Mac, nor securitize them with Ginnie Mae's guarantee, so they turned to private banks and financial firms who created so-called "private label" securitizations to raise money (Langley 2008, 155).[7]

Since these loans were not FHA insured, private label MBS didn't have the guarantee of GSE securitizations. Private securitizers came up with several mechanisms to address this risk. First, their MBS offerings would be structured with tranches, meaning they were separated into bonds of different durations, with the least risky receiving the earliest payments, and the riskiest getting the latest (Hyman 2011; MacKenzie 2011). Second, they added multiple forms of credit enhancement such as overcollateralization (buying more collateral than the face value of issued securities) and excess spread (projecting more income than necessary to meet bond obligations) (Benmelech and Dlugosz 2009). Finally, securitizers got credit ratings agencies Moody's, S&P, or Fitch to give a credit rating to each tranche of a deal, much like they would for corporate bonds. These ratings gave investors an estimate of the risk of any given tranche, which, while not a government guarantee, made these securities easier to assess and sell (MacKenzie 2011, 1794).[8]

Private securitization gained speed from the mid-1990s to the mid-2000s, exactly when two additional developments were taking place: the dual rise of subprime lending and structured mortgage finance. Private-label securitizations grew from less than a quarter of total securitizations in the 2000 to more than half by 2007 ("US Mortgage Related" 2019). In 1994 subprime mortgage lending accounted for 5 percent of originations; by 2005 it was 20 percent (Gramlich 2007, 6). But it is structured finance that grew and changed the most. Private-label securitizations went from simple, two-tranche structures to deals that involved up to twenty tranches (United States 2011). And most important for this study, a structured instrument from the world of corporate finance—collateralized debt obligations (CDOs)—was adapted into the mortgage world in the late 1990s. Banks first used CDOs to off-load the risk of multiple corporate loans from their balance sheets. Much like tranched MBS, CDOs gather together multiple corporate loans and sell tranches of the pool to investors. The investors then receive both the payments to those loans and their risk of default, in exchange for up-front capital and a clean balance sheet to the original bank lender (Jarrow 2012).

In the world of corporate loans, CDOs were used to raise capital and reduce regulatory burdens. Whole loans required relatively high reserve capital. Securitized loans required less, so securitizing loans generated capital and reduced that regulatory burden (Goodman 2002). But it was also quickly evident that CDOs could generate outright profit, because "investors would buy their tranches at spreads that were sufficiently low that the aggregate flow of cash to those investors was less than the income generated by the loans in the CDO's pool, so generating an arbitrage" (MacKenzie 2011, 1801). According to Vinod Kothari (2006), balance sheet CDOs are deals constructed in order to liquidate assets held on the balance sheet of a bank, often for the same reason as first order securitizations: to sell off risky loans and thereby reduce regulatory capital. Arbitrage CDOs are usually created by firms for the purpose of capturing the difference in the rate of interest collected on the (risky, high-yield) collateral debt of the CDO and the rate of interest paid on the CDO securities. In other words, bundling and reselling a pool of loans as securities that paid a lower yield than the interest received on the original loans netted an excess that could be appropriated.

Collateralized debt obligations moved from the world of corporate finance to mortgage finance in the mid-1990s, when the first asset-backed CDOs were created (MacKenzie 2011). As private-label MBS grew throughout the 1980s and 1990s, the market was flooded with the lower, riskier tranches of these deals, which made excellent collateral for CDOs, together with home equity loans, auto loans, and credit card receivables. By 2004 "it was common for three-quarters or more of the pool [of a CDO] to consist of subprime mortgage-backed securities" (1810). Between 2004 and 2008, over $1.5 trillion in asset-backed CDOs were issued, and 86 percent of them were arbitrage motivated (Benmelech and Dlugosz 2009, 621). Arbitrage CDOs, especially those backed by subprime MBS, were so popular because of the structural conditions that made them a money machine.

The Anatomy of CDO Arbitrage

As described above, private-label subprime MBS were tranched instruments. The highest tranches—referred to as senior—got first priority in receiving the income from the collateral, that is, the underlying mortgages. If default occurred, they were least likely to be impacted. The highest tranches were therefore considered low risk and, like any other financial security, paid a correspondingly low interest rate or yield due to the axiom of risk and return. Lower tranches—referred to as mezzanine, junior, and equity—were riskier, because in the "waterfall" (see figure 5.3) of tranches, these lower ones would absorb losses from default during their longer terms. This risk was compensated by a higher yield. The higher rate of return was meant to compensate investors for taking on the risk of losses due to potential default.

The risk of subprime MBS was assessed by the same credit ratings agencies that graded more traditional forms of debt such as sovereign and corporate bonds. Credit ratings have been relied on by financial regulators and investors since the 1930s, but the Securities and Exchange Commission (SEC)

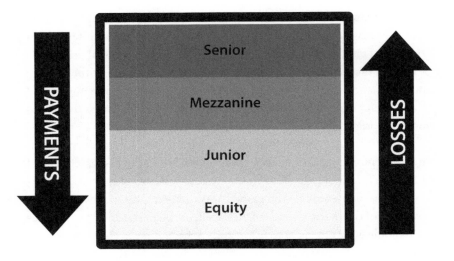

FIGURE 5.3 The waterfall of CDO payments (adapted from Jarrow 2012).

officially designated Moody's, s&p, and Fitch as nationally recognized statistical rating organizations in 1975 (United States 2011, 119). Financial market participants use credit ratings as a shortcut to risk analysis, assuming a
certain level of risk inheres in securities with a certain rating. This assumption justifies the interest rates that investors will find acceptable. Low-rated
securities must compensate investors with high returns since their rating
indicates they carry higher risk. High-rated securities are low risk and thus
may deliver lower returns. The credit ratings agencies bring the axiom of
risk and return to life.

During the go-go years of the subprime CDO arbitrage, ratings agencies
assessed the risk to each tranche of MBS and assigned it a grade on the
same scale as traditional bonds (AAA is safest followed by AA+, AA, AA−,
A+, A, A−, BBB+, BBB, and so on all the way to CCC+).[9] They used advanced
mathematical models to predict the likelihood of default for each pool of
mortgages that was securitized and then predict the level of default each
tranche could withstand with the specific credit enhancements of that particular deal (Benmelech and Dlugosz 2009). The component mortgages
of private-label securitizations were usually risky, non-FHA loans but they
were also geographically diverse, and mortgages historically defaulted at
very low rates, so the models used by ratings agencies suggested that, while
some mortgages in a pool would default, the majority would not.[10] Thus,
a large proportion, typically around 80 percent, of the resultant securities

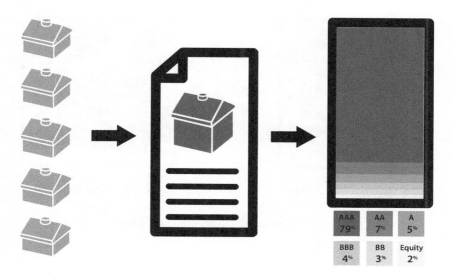

FIGURE 5.4 Typical subprime mortgage securitization (proportions taken from Ashcraft and Schuermann 2008, 30).

were rated super safe or AAA (United States 2011, 72). See figure 5.4 for an illustration of this process. Individual subprime mortgage loans are collected together into a large pool of future cash flows. These cash flows are separated into tranches, each of which is rated based on its estimated default risk. The senior tranche highest on the "waterfall" receives the highest rating, reflecting the notion that it is least likely to be affected by default (Jarrow 2012). The deal illustrated is typical in that nearly 80 percent (79 percent in this case) of the resultant securities are rated AAA.

Arbitrage CDOs were created using the lower-rated tranches of these subprime MBS deals. Unlike early corporate balance sheet CDOs, arbitrage CDOs were formed when a special purpose vehicle created by a bank or financial firm bought risky debt in financial markets to construct a collateral pool against which it would issue bonds. The first arbitrage CDOs used junk bonds—high-risk, high-yield corporate debt—as collateral. But the volume and diversity of deals quickly grew to involve many other kinds of debt including subprime MBS but also home equity loans, credit card debt, student loans, corporate debt, and even other CDO securities (MacKenzie 2011).

Like subprime MBS, CDO securities are also tranched according to their sensitivity to default and these tranches are given ratings by credit ratings agencies. Also, like subprime MBS, a large proportion of CDO securities,

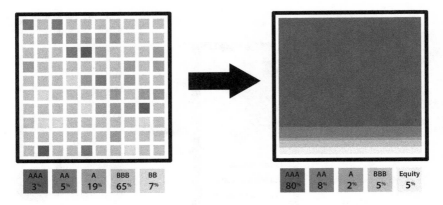

FIGURE 5.5   Typical multisector collateralized debt obligation (proportions taken from Covey et al. 2006).

70 to 80 percent, gained the highest possible credit rating of AAA (United States 2011, 127). Figure 5.5 illustrates a typical, multisector CDO deal (the collateral includes home equity loans, residential MBS, and low-rated securities from other CDOs). The average risk rating of the collateral pool (left) is BBB (mezzanine), while the average risk rating of the CDO securities is AAA (senior).

Ratings agencies knew that the collateral pools of CDOs contained high risk debt, but using the same mathematical models as they employed to rate first-round subprime MBS, the agencies rated these diversified CDO securities as mostly super safe. Benmelech and Dlugosz (2009) describe the CDO ratings process as a form of alchemy, since low-rated securities went into the collateral pool and high-rated securities came out. That alchemy quite literally turned junk, that is, low-rated securities, into senior, AAA-rated securities. The resultant AAA CDOs paid a much lower yield than the collateral received. Therefore, a large difference or spread between the interest received on the high-yield collateral and the low yield paid on the majority AAA-rated CDOs constituted the arbitrage profit for these deals.

The 2006 Lehman Brothers brochure on which figure 5.4 is based illustrates exactly how CDO arbitrage occurs (Covey et al. 2006). The collateral pool of the CDO deal receives an average interest rate of Libor plus 180 basis points (bp) (1.8 percent). The CDOs liabilities—the securities issued to investors—were nearly all rated AAA, so they pay a much lower yield, on average Libor plus 49 bp. The "gross excess spread" is thus 131 bp. After the fees deducted by the originating firm (27 bp), a "net excess spread" of 104 bp exists on the deal. This excess is delivered to the holder of the lowest, riskiest tranche. The equity tranche, as it is called, is so risky that it is not rated; any defaults will impact the equity tranche. While rated tranches are compensated with a yield that is both attractive enough to incentivize investors but also is commensurate with their relative risk, the highly risky and unrated equity tranche is compensated with the entire excess spread. Equity generally takes up 3 to 8 percent of the face value of a CDO deal (Kothari 2006, 423). Despite its small pay-in, the equity receives around a 20 percent return on investment due to the net excess spread. This return is extremely large compared to other investments (the average annual return on the S&P 500 between 2000 and 2005—the biggest boom years of subprime CDO arbitrage—was nearly flat at 0.16 percent) ("S&P 500").

The arbitrage in subprime CDOs exists in the equity or first loss tranche (United States 2011, 71). As Vinod Kothari explains, this is not a real arbitrage, in the sense that it does not adhere to the strict economic definition: "The term 'arbitrage' is loosely used . . . *Arbitrage* in the sense used here means trying to capture via active management the spread between the return on assets and funding costs" (Kothari 2006). As noted above, the profit comes to the equity tranche only if defaults on the underlying pool of debt do not occur. If they do, and in great enough proportion, the entire return to the equity tranche can be wiped out. As we learned in the 2007 financial crisis, defaults can reach the more senior tranches as well. This indeed appears to be more of a gamble, what Henry Crosby Emery would term "time-speculation" (1896, 137). What's more, the 2006 Lehman Brothers brochure referenced earlier was attempting to convince investors to take equity positions in its CDOs (Covey et al. 2006). In chapter 3, I argue that financial traders aggressively and jealously pursue arbitrage for themselves at the expense of all other market participants. It is therefore highly unlikely that Lehman would graciously offer a 20 percent return to its investors if it believed it could secure that return for itself risk free.

However, there are reasons to consider the subprime CDOs that were created in great numbers in the early 2000s arbitrage trades. First, they were highly profitable. Although investment firms are not forthcoming with details of their arbitrage operations, there is evidence that the subprime mortgage CDO arbitrage trade netted billions in profits to arbitrageurs in the early 2000s. Arbitrage in CDOs during that time netted profits of "over 40 per cent" according to one participant in the deals (MacKenzie 2012, 341). The Securities Industry and Financial Markets Association (SIFMA) estimates that over $1 trillion worth of arbitrage CDOs were issued between 2005 and 2007 ("Global CDO Issuance" 2015). An estimate of the arbitrage in these three years alone, based on the Lehman deal, would indicate that they netted over $10 billion in profit, not including fees. In 2010 *ProPublica* detailed the activities of Magnetar Capital, a hedge fund that began aggressively buying up CDO equity in the spring of 2006, on the very edge of the credit crunch that would dissolve into the financial crisis.[11] By one estimate, they held one-third to one-half of CDO equity tranches at that time, meaning that they were engaging in arbitrage by receiving the net excess spread on a huge proportion of CDO deals. According to the *Wall Street Journal*, this single fund made over $2 billion in 2007.[12]

Second, the trades relied on price stabilization—in this case created by structural inequalities in the market—to profit, as all arbitrage trades must. In the case of subprime CDO arbitrage, the structural difference that constituted arbitrage profit was between the two interest rates. The interest rate stabilization that secured the CDO arbitrage profit as a continuous money machine was sedimented by the alchemy of CDO credit rating. The formulas used by credit rating agencies that rated CDOs as mostly AAA set up a structural difference between the interest rate received on the CDO collateral and the yield paid on the CDO securities, allowing an arbitrage trade that continuously pumped out profits instead of closing over time due to the forces of supply and demand. In other words, they were money machines. Robert Jarrow explains how this worked: "CDOs and CDO^2 were created to take advantage of market mispricings caused by the misratings of structured debt. . . . The trading of these market mispricings should have increased the informational efficiency of debt markets, as the impact of the trades removed the arbitrage opportunities. But in this case, the *institutional structures* . . . enabled the mispricings to persist. As such, these securities facilitated a massive transfer of wealth from financial institutions who overly relied on the credit ratings to the CDO and CDO^2 equity holders in hedge funds and investment banks" (2012, 2, my emphasis).

Because the equity tranche is the first loss piece of a CDO, the one that receives income last—perhaps as late as five or six years after the first payments on collateral come in—purchasing it doesn't seem to fit the economic definition of arbitrage as a trade that nets a certain, riskless profit. The equity holder must wait for repayment due to its position at the bottom of the waterfall. However, as I explained, real-life arbitrage can occur over time, as long as instantaneity is simulated through differential advantages in communication networks or the use of derivatives. In the case of CDO arbitrage, this was done using credit default swap (CDS) contracts, which first emerged to address the same goals as CDOs of reducing the risk of default and reducing regulatory capital. Unlike corporate bonds, which are issued and tradable in more or less liquid markets, many corporate loans made by banks were not generally resalable or tradable (Tett 2009). If banks wanted to reduce their risk and regulatory capital, they had to find a way to do it without actually selling the loan off their balance sheet. Credit default swaps allowed banks to sell the risk of default to investors for a regular payment. If default occurred, the investors would be required to pay the bank the lost value. If default did not occur, investors kept the payments made over the life of the contract for a tidy profit. Credit default swap contracts had the basic features of insurance protection—premium-driven payments and event-triggered payouts. Regulators endorsed the insurance logic of the contracts and allowed banks to reduce their regulatory capital accordingly (Tett 2009).

Magnetar hedged their position by shorting the next closest mezzanine tranches with credit default swaps. This meant that if the CDO succeeded, they would receive the high return on equity, and if it failed, they would receive payments from their CDS. In other words, they secured profit regardless of default, by buying low and selling high, and using stabilizing derivatives contracts. What's more, despite its long duration, commentators have described Magnetar's trade as arbitrage. There is no reason to think that other holders of CDO equity did not similarly hedge their positions to create a trade that fits the definition of arbitrage in real life. Therefore, these arbitrage CDOs—as their name suggests—were well and truly money machine arbitrage instruments.

Throughout the early 2000s, the use of CDS increased, particularly when they referenced mortgage-backed securities, thus allowing investors and firms to bet on the probability of default of these instruments. Credit default swaps were also used to create synthetic CDOs that weren't constructed by buying up actual debt, but rather by selling credit default swaps on mortgage-backed securities that the firm didn't itself own. Based on the assumption that credit default swaps accurately priced the risk of default on underlying securities, the securitizing firm could sell investors a tranched portion of CDS premiums, rather than the actual MBS themselves. Investors would receive regular CDS premium payments in place of interest payments on a traditional CDO and would only lose their principal in the event of a default (just like a traditional CDO). Synthetic CDOs reduced the amount of capital needed to make a CDO arbitrage profit, and thus became even more popular than cash CDOs (Goodman 2002).

The production of cash and synthetic CDOs delivered continuous prof-its until the bursting of the housing bubble reversed the long period of housing appreciation into a contraction, and the structural conditions—appreciation of housing prices and high credit ratings—that allowed sub-prime CDO arbitrage to produce profit evaporated. The investors who bought CDO tranches containing subprime mortgages and the firms who sold CDS protection on them lost enormous amounts of money. Some of the largest U.S. banks, hedge funds, and insurers were among the sellers and investors. The U.S. government bailed out the firms that did not fold and the country, and world, were thrown into a protracted recession that foreclosed millions of homes, evaporated retirement savings, eliminated jobs, and stagnated wages (United States 2011). Money machine arbitrage in subprime CDOs proliferated securities whose profitability relied on—like all money machines—structural conditions to maintain the spread. When those conditions changed, subprime MBS and CDOs became "toxic."

CDO arbitrage is financial capture at its finest; bankers and hedge fund managers appropriating value with esoteric instruments fully justified by financial theory claimed they helped better distribute risk and return when, in actuality, they served to secure a greater proportion of profit to those ar-bitrageurs who had the resources, knowledge, and networks to carry it out. But the reasons for its success are far from clear. In order for the apparatus of capture to function, more and more arbitrage CDOs had to be created. This required a steady flow of subprime mortgage debt, the alchemy of credit ratings that could transform that risky debt into safe investments, and investors to demand more and more AAA-rated CDO securities. Each of these conditions seems at the very least contingent, if not downright irrational. Why would borrowers choose to pay exorbitant interest rates to purchase a home? Why would credit ratings agencies give subprime MBS and CDOs such high ratings? Why would investors rush to purchase these securities in such large amounts?

The answers to these questions are found in the intricate ways that the abstract domination of risk played out during the run-up to the crisis, at multiple levels in contemporary U.S. life. Both borrowing for housing and investing by institutional investors constructed the context in which CDO arbitrage could take place. In the next chapter, I explore the ways that the axioms of risk and return and risk measurement were actualized within this context.

SIX

The Emperor's New Clothes

The Financial Crisis Inquiry Commission (FCIC) reported that "in 2007, 20 percent of U.S. CDO securities would be downgraded. In 2008, 91 percent would" (United States 2011, 148). In other words, 91 percent of collateralized debt obligations (CDOs) revealed themselves to be riskier than their original credit ratings suggested. The "alchemy" of subprime CDO arbitrage was revealed to be a farce (Benmelech and Dlugosz 2009). Yet the question remains of how exactly that alchemy was produced not as a scandal or fraud, but as a fully understood, regulator-sanctioned financial activity right up to the point that it crippled the credit system and caused the Great Recession. Some economists and sociologists (e.g., Acharya et al. 2009; MacKenzie 2011) have argued that errors and inefficiencies in the construction of financial markets led to the crisis. This dominant interpretation can also be found in the FCIC's authoritative report on the crisis (United States 2011). The FCIC authors claim that executive pay structures at investment banks "had the unintended consequence of creating incentives to increase both risk and leverage, which could lead to larger jumps in a company's stock" (63). They also argue that the "originate-to-distribute" model of mortgage origination, wherein brokers sell mortgages to Wall Street securitizers rather than holding them on their own balance sheets as banks and thrifts traditionally did, promoted perverse incentives to create risky, poorly underwritten loans (89). This discourse sets up a dichotomy between efficient markets and the period of subprime CDO arbitrage as if the latter were a momentary, pathological exception to the efficient market rule. It suggests that if perverse incentives can be corrected and right risk measurements taken, finance will return to its main function of allocating resources and risk in the most efficient and beneficial distribution possible.

Popular commentators have been more aggressive in identifying not market efficiency issues, but individual or collective boogeymen, ranging from greedy financial executives to rent-seeking credit ratings agents to dissimulating borrowers, as the ultimate culprits. Popular narratives suggest that greed and power led rich, white financial professionals and government officials to commit fraud of epic proportions on ordinary Americans (*Inside Job* 2011; Taibbi 2010). These popular accounts take better aim at the harm that finance has done than economists' reactions, but also overpersonalize the power relations of finance, offering individual targets for justifiable frustration and outrage, but giving up on broader systematic explanations of how finance not only allows but also compels not just financial executives but ordinary folks to participate in a system that harms many people.

In this chapter, I reexamine the causes of the crisis through the capture framework as a way to account for both the systematic nature of financial capitalism and its consequences. This framework centers on arbitrage as the form of capture in finance, and therefore reframes the question of the crisis as one not of market structure or individual greed, but as one of abstract domination, the "social universe of abstract objective constraints that function in a lawlike fashion" (Postone 1993, 163). Viewing subprime CDO arbitrage as capture leads to the question of how the "objective constraints" of the risk axioms functioned in everyday life to produce the conditions of possibility of CDO arbitrage.

Axioms and Alchemy

The axiom of risk and return encapsulates the notion that reward only comes to those who put something on the line. It suggests that the higher the risk of a security, whether measured as variance, implied volatility, or credit rating, the higher return investors will demand in order to buy that security. The axiom of risk measurement asserts that risk is a quantifiable fact that can be empirically measured. Together, these axioms underpin the risk-based pricing that allowed mortgage brokers to charge subprime borrowers more in interest and the alchemy that constituted subprime arbitrage CDOs (Benmelech and Dlugosz 2009). Borrowers' supposedly objective credit scores showed that they were risky and, therefore, they received higher interest rates on their mortgages to remunerate lenders with more return for being willing to take the risk. Securitizing risky pieces of mortgage-backed securities into a new issue of tranched CDO securities could only yield a profit if these securities were rated well enough by credit agencies that their yield was far less than the subprime interest payments being received on their collateral.

In the next two sections, I explore the social relations that constituted the "quasi-objective" social mediation of financial capitalism in the run-up to the crisis, using these two axioms as analytical frames through which to rethink the causes of the crisis (Postone 1993, 5). First, I explore the processes that led to subprime CDOs getting high, AAA credit ratings, and the institutional structures and practices that led investors to buy as many as securitizers could make. I show how each of these axioms made the securitization and investing processes seem not just rational, but necessary, despite the ex post facto critiques of many parties involved.

The second section examines the story of subprime mortgage lending through the lens of these two axioms. It tells the story of subprime lending as one in which risk measurement attempted to fix the problem of gender and racial exclusion from consumer credit markets. However, in conjunction with the axiom of risk and return, and the changing culture of homeownership, subprime mortgage lending, at least initially, joined racial capture to the abstract domination of risk that allowed subprime CDO arbitrage to take place.

THE ALCHEMY OF CREDIT RATINGS

Credit ratings of both the collateral and the CDO securities were essential for the arbitrage in subprime CDOs to take place. The "alchemy," as Benmelech and Dlugosz (2009) describe it, that allowed low rated MBS to go into the collateral pool and high rated CDO bonds to come out is thus worthy of scrutiny (see figure 5.5).

The CDO securities were given high ratings, which meant they could pay lower yields. But since they were made up of high-risk, high-yield collateral, they could offer slightly higher yields than other AAA securities, drawing the "giant pool of money" circulating in the early 2000s to invest heavily in subprime CDOs ("Giant Pool" 2008). Additionally, as Benmelech and Dlugosz explain, "extensive use of credit ratings in the regulation of financial institutions created a natural clientele for CDO . . . securities" (2009, 631). They continue: "At least 44 SEC rules and forms incorporated agency ratings as of June 2008. Minimum capital requirements at banks, insurance companies, and broker-dealers depend on the credit ratings of the assets on their balance sheets. Pension funds, a $10 trillion source of capital in the United States, also face ratings-based regulations. . . . This matrix of regulation creates institutional demand for highly rated securities" (630–31).

In some cases, such as for pension funds, institutional demand for these securities derived from a combination of risk aversion and reliance on credit ratings as a proxy for risk. For banks, regulations themselves incentivized the purchase of AAA-rated securities. Under the Basel Accords, whole loans, especially risky subprime loans, require banks to hold back a relatively large proportion of their cash (around 5 percent) to cover potential losses. Banks would rather have as little capital in reserve as possible so that they can lend and receive fees and interest on those funds. The Basel Accord system weights AAA-rated bonds as less risky. Thus, by simply switching out a portfolio of whole, subprime loans for AAA-rated MBS or CDOs, a bank could reduce its regulatory capital by as much as 20 percent (Benmelech and Dlugosz 2009). Banks still had loan collateral on their books in the form of MBS and CDOs, but they freed up a significant proportion of capital previously held for losses.[1]

The widespread acceptance of credit ratings as an adequate measure of the riskiness of bonds—a reflection of the axiom of risk measurement— drove institutional investors to demand highly rated bonds. Additionally, CDOs were far more abundant than other AAA securities. Benmelech and Dlugosz (2009) claim that, despite high "institutional demand for highly rated securities . . . the supply of highly rated single-name securities is fairly limited. For example, only five nonfinancial companies and a few sovereigns had AAA ratings as of 2007" (631). So CDOs that transformed difficult-to-sell yet abundant mezzanine tranches of subprime MBS and other asset-backed securities into 80 percent AAA-rated bonds found almost unlimited demand from investors. Securitizers could then price the 80 percent of their CDOs that received a AAA rating much lower than the yield they received on the collateral, because of the axiom of risk and return. The axioms of risk measurement and risk and return conspired to turn credit ratings into the key levers of financial capture in subprime CDO arbitrage.

It is clear that credit ratings contributed to the "CDO machine," the housing bubble, and therefore the financial crisis (United States 2011, 127).

Especially after credit rating agency executives testified before Congress that their ratings were "opinions" (*Inside Job* 2011), public and scholarly scrutiny fell upon their practices. People wanted to know how securities that would become, during the crisis, severely devalued and toxic were rated AAA in such large numbers. Some have cited "ratings shopping" as the cause of the high ratings given to CDOS.[2] Issuers of securities pay credit rating agencies to rate their deals. Matthew Richardson and Lawrence White explain that this "issuer pays" model incentivizes securitizers to shop for the best rating among the three major agencies: S&P, Moody's, and Fitch (2009, 104). Credit rating agencies have been blamed for offering high ratings to attract business within this model, leading to inflated ratings of risky securities. The financial crisis seems to have borne out this suspicion with the massive downgrading of MBS and CDOs from AAA to lower ratings, resulting in write-downs that caused a downward spiral to bankruptcy or bailout for many banks and financial firms.

However, proving that the agencies had incentive to operate in a particular way does not prove that they did in fact do so. Donald MacKenzie's (2011) study of credit raters' formulas actually looks at the historical and sociological foundations of CDO ratings. MacKenzie argues that the financial crisis occurred because financial participants were not able to construct adequate knowledge about the systematic risk of mortgage defaults during the inflationary period of the housing bubble. In particular, he blames the two-step organizational division within credit rating agencies in which MBS are first rated for likelihood of default and then, in another organizational location, CDOs containing tranches of these MBS are evaluated. He explains that credit rating agencies produced estimates of MBS default risk by running stress scenarios and imposing ratings penalties on geographically concentrated pools. CDO rating was done by wholly different groups of raters, those who rated corporate CDOs rather than those who rated MBS (1815). This fact is of major significance for MacKenzie because of the difference between corporate debt and mortgage-backed CDOs. He explains: "A corporate bond or loan will typically be high in idiosyncratic risk, hence the justification of giving higher ratings to tranches formed from a diversified pool of such bonds or loans than to its components. [MBS], however, often no longer contained much idiosyncratic risk that could be diversified away, but only systematic risk (exposure to common factors such as the risk of nationwide house price decline) that was not greatly reduced by packaging [MBS] into a pool" (1815). The application of the same model used to estimate default risk in corporate CDOs—known as the Guassian copula formula—to subprime mortgage-backed CDOs thus represented, for MacKenzie, a serious problem in the construction of knowledge about the risk of the latter.

MacKenzie (2011) holds out this quirk in the rating of subprime CDOs as evidence that the credit rating agencies got the risk calculation wrong. Unlike critics who blame rating shopping, MacKenzie blames organizational conditions of knowledge production. But implicit in both critiques is the assumption that risk *could be* accurately measured; it just wasn't. In other words, the axiom of risk measurement underpins even the critiques of the credit rating process. MacKenzie shies away from arguing that raters incorrectly assessed the risk specifically to allow the arbitrage in CDOs to take place, saying "I have found no clear evidence that they saw the danger of [MBS] CDOs and ignored it for the sake of fees. On the contrary, the evaluation of [MBS] CDOs using existing corporate CDO models and similar correlation values is plausibly interpretable as organizational routine" (1830–31). I would extend his interpretation even further, however, to argue—using evidence from his study—that the raters were actually acting cautiously within the objective constraint of the axiom of risk measurement.

The Guassian copula formula used to measure correlation between securities in the collateral pools of CDOs required an input in the form of a "correlation parameter" that had to be supplied by the rater (MacKenzie 2011, 1814). MacKenzie makes much of the fact that raters ended up using a correlation parameter adopted from the world of corporate CDOs rather than getting the correct input for the mortgage-backed security market. Raters assumed that default risk for MBS CDOs was diversified away in the same way that it was for corporate CDOs. Specifically, Fitch's, Moody's, and S&P used the default correlation input of 0.3, the same number "used for corporations in the same industry," to evaluate the risk of subprime MBS CDOs (1811). Only with this input could the majority of subprime MBS CDOs be rated AAA by these agencies. Once they were labeled with AAA ratings, these securities based on high risk, high yield, subprime collateral could pay relatively low yields to investors, enabling the arbitrage profit. MacKenzie points out that if raters had used a higher correlation, then there would have been no arbitrage opportunities. He references a 2006 thought experiment run by "some CDO specialists at one of the rating agencies," which found, through some simple math and case-by-case evaluation, that a better correlation figure for MBS CDOs would have been much higher, 0.8, a figure that would have prevented CDO arbitrage from occurring and also, potentially, the bubble and bust in the housing market (1818). MacKenzie uses this vignette to suggest that the separate evaluation of MBS and MBS CDOs, along with the convention of using the corporate correlation number, made the diversification of each pool seem greater than it actually was. The underlying argument here is that if these knowledge-making practices had been done correctly, an accurate measurement of risk would have been made. The market would have been efficient and all of this pain could have been avoided.

However, this ex post facto speculation again obscures the rationality of the system in which 0.3 was selected as the correlation parameter. In the very same paper, MacKenzie notes that the "choice of 0.3 as the intra-sectoral [MBS] asset correlation could actually be interpreted as cautious, more cautious, at least in the case of mortgages, than a purely econometric estimate: Parisi (2004) reports an average correlation of 0.06 of the losses on pairs of pools of U.S. residential mortgages in the period 1995–2002" (1814). Therefore, the use of 0.3, a number five times larger than the empirical data suggested, was seen by some at the time as "overly conservative" (Chen et al. 2005, 3n, qtd. in MacKenzie 2011, 1814). Indeed, credit raters could have pointed to the data to use 0.06 as the correlation parameter, making the arbitrage even more profitable. That they did not supports the idea that at the time, ex ante, risk measurement was not so much wrong as just plain arbitrary.

The most important thing was not *what* risk measurement was used, but *that* risk was measurable in the first place. With risk measurements in hand, arbitrageurs could create a comparison that produced capture. It was not the avarice or suboptimal knowledge-making processes that directed the flows of subprime mortgages into the CDO machine, but rather the system of abstract domination organized by the very notion that risk could be measured.[3] That is not to say that, especially toward the end of the housing bubble in 2006 and 2007, some companies, including Goldman Sachs, Merrill Lynch, and Countrywide Financial, did not issue MBS and CDOs that they knew were riskier than they represented to their customers and regulators. There is excellent evidence that they did just that (United States 2011, 193; O'Hara 2016, 86–87). But these overtly deceptive practices came late in the game, after the bubble had grown large enough to create a crisis, and after billions of dollars in arbitrage profits had already been made with legitimate risk measurements. In the next section, I examine the ways that the axioms of risk and return and risk measurement, along with another form of capture, produced those subprime mortgage payments that flowed into the CDO machine in the run-up to the financial crisis.

One could choose any number of starting points to tell the story of subprime lending in the United States. In some ways, its roots lie in the transatlantic slave trade and the cultural production of race as a form of social mediation and abstract domination. Despite multiple changes to American capitalism since the official end of slavery, the abstract domination of race continues to support capitalist capture. Jodi Melamed explains: "As capitalist social relations change, race remains a procedure that justifies the nongeneralizability of capitalist wealth" (2006, 10). That nongeneralizability is evident in the racial dynamics of credit. According to Gary Dymski, Jesus Hernandez, and Lisa Mohanty (2013), Black borrowers were much more likely to receive subprime mortgages than white borrowers in the years before the crisis. This fact is a result of the marriage of the abstract domination of race and the abstract domination of risk in the subprime lending that contributed to the financial crisis.

The longer history of mortgage lending demonstrates how deeply race and risk are imbricated in the U.S. consumer credit market. In 1934 the Federal Housing Administration (FHA) was established as part of Franklin Roosevelt's New Deal in response to the Great Depression. As I explained in chapter 5, the FHA was designed to facilitate a secondary market in mortgages so that investment capital could drive an increase in homeownership. But this government scheme was actually the second initiative in the New Deal to try to address the lack of adequate housing for the masses. The Public Works Administration planned to tackle the problem by allocating nearly $500 million to building "low-cost housing and slum clearance" (Ickes 1951, qtd. in Hyman 2011, 51). However, this direct intervention by the government angered the business community and was eventually abandoned (Hyman 2011). The secondary mortgage market that the FHA facilitated instead touched off the dynamics that eventually led to subprime CDO arbitrage by connecting mortgage borrowers to investors through financial circuits.

The combination of strict building guidelines laid out in the FHA *Underwriting Manual*, FHA mortgage insurance, and mortgage resale facilitated by the Federal National Mortgage Association (Fannie Mae) did exactly what it was designed to do; it supercharged the housing market and dramatically increased homeownership, but mostly among white families. Black borrowers were systemically excluded and exploited within the new mortgage system. Multiple policies explicitly and surreptitiously prevented Black Americans from borrowing to buy homes (Hyman 2011). The FHA *Underwriting Manual* ratified the practice of "redlining," whereby neighborhoods of Black families were drawn out of mortgage lending. It also directed homeowners to use racial covenants—home sale contract riders that prevented buyers from reselling to Black people or other minorities—to prevent Black people from moving into their neighborhoods (Baradaran 2017, 105).

The impact of these policies on long-term racial segregation and Black wealth cannot be understated. Malini Ranganathan (2016) explains:

> Perhaps no other public institutions were more responsible for solidifying housing inequality in America for decades to come than the Home Owners Loan Corporation (HOLC) and the Federal Housing Administration (FHA), both of which were signed into order in the early 1930s by President Roosevelt at the height of the Great Depression. Both institutions were charged with reviving the depression-hit housing industry by refinancing and insuring loans to certain worthy individuals and rendering loans more costly or refusing them altogether to other devalued individuals. In city after city, from Ferguson to Flint, the FHA not only insured loans overwhelmingly to whites but also subsidized the construction of entire white suburbs by guaranteeing financing to builders that excluded African-Americans, "aliens," and other minorities. (24)

The FHA made its manual race neutral in the 1940s and forbade racial covenants, but they continued to be used informally for decades. Similarly, banks continued redlining Black neighborhoods and denying loans in them up into the present ("Struggle for Black" 2018). Additionally, "racially coded geographic terms such as 'compatibility among neighborhood occupants' and 'harmonious neighborhoods' continued to be used for loan insurance purposes" into the present as well (Rothstein 2014, qtd. in Ranganathan 2016, 24).

However, it would be wrong to see this as a story merely of exclusion. As Hyman (2011) explains, Black families did buy homes in the years after the FHA was established, but they paid more to do so. Black households held less wealth, received less income, and therefore borrowed more, when they could get a loan, to buy a house in the suburbs. They also paid higher rates of interest. What's more, white mortgage borrowing was subsidized by Black dollars. Savings deposited in Black banks were often funneled into government securities; Black banks were less well capitalized and experienced higher defaults, so they were required by regulators to hold more

Treasury bonds. But this mean that Black savings thereby indirectly funded programs like FHA loans that rarely benefited Black borrowers (Baradaran 2017; Towns and Hardin 2018).

The result of this stratified evolution in mortgage borrowing was a two-path system. White borrowers attained the American Dream and accumulated wealth in the form of home equity, subsidized by the government through low interest rates and facilitated through the secondary mortgage market that funneled investment dollars into mortgage lending. Black borrowers were excluded from borrowing or paid more, creating a decades-long wealth deficit that reinforced their second-class status in American society.

In the 1960s and 1970s, several changes to credit markets conspired to change Black people's limited inclusion in housing markets into what Keeanga-Yamahtta Taylor (2019) calls "predatory inclusion." First, the 1968 Housing and Urban Development Act created new government guarantees for low-income mortgage loans. The loans could be a significant source of income for lenders, who wouldn't need to worry about whether they could be repaid because of their guarantee. But, also because of this guarantee, lenders had no incentive to make mortgages on quality properties. Instead, they made loans to poor Black borrowers on dilapidated homes that could be quickly foreclosed on and recycled into another mortgage.[4] This "predatory inclusion" maintained long-standing racial housing segregation and lower quality housing for Black people, but offered new avenues for profit for the real estate industry:

> By ignoring race, new practices that were intended to facilitate inclusion reinforced existing patterns of inequality and discrimination. For example, poor housing and neighborhood conditions caused by earlier FHA policies became the basis on which new lenders, in the new era of FHA colorblindness and an end to redlining, could still continue to treat potential Black homeowners differently. African American neighborhoods were given the racially neutral descriptor "subprime." . . . Though race was apparently no longer a factor, its cumulative effect had already marked Black neighborhoods in such ways that still made them distinguishable and vulnerable to new forms of financial manipulation. Inclusion was possible, but on predatory and exploitative terms. (K. Taylor 2019, 18)

This changed the relationship between the abstract domination of race and the abstract domination of risk. As Taylor puts it, "In an earlier era, risk had been the pretext for excluding potential Black homeowners; by the late 1960s, risk made Black buyers attractive. In fact, the riskier the buyer, the better" (2019, 18).

Second, race riots after Martin Luther King Jr.'s assassination placed the economic condition of Black ghettos on the national stage, and led Congress to debate ways to alleviate the situation. Many proposals were made, including increasing Black ownership of ghetto businesses, especially banks, increasing investment in ghettos, and establishing community credit unions in Black neighborhoods. But the Fair Credit Reporting Act (1970/1973) and Equal Credit Opportunity Act (1974/1976) were the measures that came to favor in the end. These laws made it illegal to use subjective criteria or secret data to make credit decisions, or to discriminate against borrowers based on identity characteristics (Hyman 2011).

The problem, of course, was that these laws sidestepped "the more fundamental question of how economic structures, not individual character, made borrowers creditworthy" in the name of democratizing credit (Hyman 2011, 216). Legislators believed that "credit has been and continues to be the cornerstone upon which our enviable U.S. standard of living rests" and thought that increasing access to it would undoubtedly improve the standard of living for Black Americans (Millstein 1972, qtd. in Hyman 2011, 191). But instead of addressing structural issues, these laws were implemented through technocratic solutions using recently computerized credit bureaus—the Credit Data Corporation was the first computerized credit bureau in 1965 (Langley 2008)—and mathematical underwriting formulas. Loan officers were replaced by automated decisions made on the basis of supposedly objective credit files and—importantly—risk models. Risk measurement became the new standard around which credit decisions were made. As a non-identity-based characteristic, risk seemed like both a fair way to discriminate between borrowers and a rational and necessary parameter for lenders to consider. When Fair, Isaac and Company (FICO) introduced the generic credit bureau model that would become the ubiquitous FICO score in 1989, the axiom of risk measurement came into full flower (Lauer 2017).

Hyman (2011) points out that merely excluding race and gender from underwriting formulas does not account for the historical, geographical, and cultural factors that make Black people and women earn less income and have less wealth. So credit risk modeling distributes such groups across the lower end of the "fair" scale of credit scores. This creation of neutral credit scores is an instance of what Jodi Melamed calls "neoliberal multiculturalism," in which previous, overtly racist policy is replaced by a "normative cultural model of race (which now sometimes displaces conventional racial reference altogether) as a discourse to justify inequality for some as fair or natural" (2006, 14). With this new standardization of inequality in place, the axiom of risk measurement was enshrined in law and accepted as the basis of credit underwriting, providing a new, fully rational and unexamined social mediation that could enable arbitrage capture.

The acceptance of risk measurement as the best way to make underwriting decisions ushered in a massive expansion of credit in the 1990s. As Paul Langley put it, "the seeming control over the uncertain future that credit reporting and scoring gives to lenders provides the basis for more lending to a greater number of borrowers" (2008, 151). However, the boom was not among the low-risk or prime borrowers, but rather the subprime. In order to lend to this riskier group, lenders had to figure out how to profit from them. The answer was risk-based pricing, which Langley defines as "the categorization of borrowers according to calculations as to their likelihood of default, and the charging of graduated rates of interest based on these categorizations" (164).

In theory, risk-based pricing appears to square the circle of credit exclusion by making a way for lenders to profitably lend—as they are, after all, in the business of profiting—to those who would otherwise get no credit. Donncha Marron explains: "Risk pricing is thus seen to enhance the general welfare—rewarding the low risk with low rates and allowing the high risk the opportunities of credit formerly denied to them" (2007, 122). In 2001 Senator Phil Gramm used a similar argument to shoot down congressional attempts to regulate subprime lenders (Rivlin 2010, 138). Gramm was a bank-friendly legislator famous for headlining the Gramm-Leach-Bliley Act that dismantled the Glass-Steagall Act, which placed restrictions on banks after the Great Depression. In a speech on the Senate floor, he said that "some people look at subprime lending and see evil. . . . I see the American dream in action. My mother lived it as a result of a finance company making a loan that a bank would not make" (138). Defendants of many forms of predatory lending, from payday lending to reverse redlining—the practice of targeting low-income, usually Black, homeowners with high-interest, high fee home equity loans, often ostensibly to make repairs to their homes (B. Williams 2004)—have all echoed the axiom of risk and return by arguing that riskier borrowers must pay higher rates of interest to remunerate lenders for taking them on.

The issue is that for-profit subprime lenders use the logic of risk-based pricing as a cover for charging high interest on loans that then feed the

CDO machine, rather than for making loans aimed at helping people like Gramm's mother. Martin Eakes, CEO of the nonprofit Self-Help Credit Union, which is one of the oldest subprime lenders in the country, testified before Congress in 2001 that Self-Help charged "about a half of one percent higher rate than a conventional rate mortgage" and that "we've had virtually no defaults whatsoever in 23 years" ("Predatory Lending Practices" 2001). His testimony pointedly demonstrates that subprime lending and high-interest-rate lending are not necessarily the same thing. But the axiom of risk and return justifies the latter. Subprime lending of the sort done by Self-Help Credit Union is rare. Before the crisis, subprime lending at rates more than double that of the prime rate were common (Rivlin 2010). In contrast to the inspirational image provided by Gramm, risk-based pricing has not given low-income and minority borrowers a leg up into the middle class. Instead, it has justified high-interest lending to those who could least afford it, all while leading to a boom in private securitization.

For the first fifty years, government-sponsored enterprises (GSEs) like Fannie Mae and Freddie Mac facilitated the secondary mortgage market by reselling mortgages or creating "pass-through securities" that did not skim an arbitrage profit from the securitization process. When subprime mortgage lending took off in the 1980s and 1990s, banks began to create private-label securitizations themselves, without the GSEs or the actual or implicit guarantees their securities carried. These private-label MBS allowed banks to recoup the capital they had lent, book fees for originating the mortgages, and lend again. The lower-rated tranches of these private, subprime MBS were the collateral for arbitrage CDOs.

The axiom of risk and return, in the guise of risk-based pricing, continued to give a patina of fairness and rationality to the process even while the worst mortgages—the ones that would eventually fail and create the financial crisis—were being issued. The birth of private-label MBS for securitizing subprime mortgages coincided with the first programs for promoting "minority home ownership as a long-term, structural response to the widening social inequalities of neoliberal America" under President Bill Clinton (Cooper 2017, 140). Originally conceived as a form of "asset-based welfare" that posited the appreciation of a home as a way to supplement stagnant wages for low-income Americans, the promotion of mortgage-funded homeownership for people with low credit scores in the 1990s snowballed into the subprime crisis in the 2000s. Rather than a true "democratization of credit," these programs were, from the start, tied up with the issuance of more expensive credit through risk-based pricing (140).

In 2002 President George W. Bush rolled out a new initiative to promote homeownership for low-income and minority borrowers.[5] The program would include grants through a newly established American Dream Down-Payment Fund and tax credits for builders to invest in low-cost areas. But Bush also directed Fannie Mae and Freddie Mac to "increase their commitment to minority markets by more than $440 billion" ("Home Ownership" 2011). In an echo of the racial dynamic of the HUD Act described by Taylor, what this meant in actuality was that the GSEs, which had previously held little private mortgage debt and almost no subprime debt, would begin buying subprime private-label MBS to meet goals set by Bush and HUD (Thomas and Van Order 2010).[6] The government didn't make subsidized loans directly to minority homebuyers, but rather stimulated the market in high-interest, subprime loans by buying them up in the secondary market.

Wyly et al. (2012) are careful to point out that the category of subprime isn't fully, or even predominantly, composed of minority borrowers. After subprime lending accelerated in the 1990s, it expanded into new markets: "Things changed dramatically after 2001, when the appetite for yield required volume—thus necessitating an expansion of predation into the markets of whiteness in American housing" (580). But for Black borrowers, whose risky credit scores are themselves accumulations of historical factors like redlining and Black incarceration, the effects of subprime lending tend to be more dramatic. Jacob Rugh, Len Albright, and Douglas Massey (2015) found that, for mortgages issued by Wells Fargo in Baltimore from 2000 to 2008, Black borrowers on average paid around $15,000 more for their mortgages over the life of the loan than their white counterparts of similar credit risk. Black borrowers were also more likely to experience foreclosure and, significantly, that foreclosure produced a disproportionate reduction of wealth as well (Rugh et al. 2015). It's no wonder, then, that Dymski, Hernandez, and Mohanty find that increasing minority homeownership through subprime loans did not, during the period 1995–2007, increase minority wealth, even while white borrowers did experience wealth growth (2013, 139). This is understandable given mortgage broker practices that have been revealed in lawsuits following the financial crisis. Wells Fargo was sued for targeting Black people: "Between 2004 and 2014, African American borrowers were twice as likely to receive high-cost loans when compared with white borrowers with similar credit backgrounds."[7] Black women were five times more likely to get subprime loans than white males, even controlling for creditworthiness (Servon 2017, 44).

Risk-based pricing seems logical prima facie, as much as the axiom of risk and return seems obvious and rational. But in practice, in the run-up to the financial crisis, it functioned to enforce the abstract domination of race and risk together. Risk-based pricing "[makes] inequalities appear fair" by funneling race-based differences "into categories of difference that make it possible to order, analyze, describe, and evaluate what emerges out of force relations as the permissible content of other domains of U.S. modernity (e.g., law, politics, and economy)" (Melamed 2011, 13, 11). Arbitrage in mortgage-backed CDOs only became possible when risk-based pricing and subprime lending had been established and applied disproportionately first to Black debtors and then to anyone who could be had. The spectacular success of and damage done by the subprime CDO arbitrage points to the fact that financial capture finds special synergy where the abstract domination of race and risk intensify one another, in what Malini Ranganathan calls "racial financial capitalism" (2019, 2).

Finance does not distribute risk efficiently to those most willing to bear it, it *conjures* risk. As Louise Amoore puts it, "risk is a construction, a 'way in which we govern and are governed'" (2013, 7). Through the axioms of risk measurement and risk and return, finance whips the crowd into a rousing appreciation of the emperor's new clothes. And, once all are convinced that risk is measurable and correlated to return, finance then distributes it precisely to the particular places where it can facilitate capture. That we see risk as measurable and a natural correlate of return is evidence of this new form of abstract domination in financial capitalism. Risk is not nearly as cleanly and easily measurable as finance tells us, nor is return its natural correlate. It could be otherwise. We could decide to reward caution, equality, or collective decision making. One might argue that we should not, but that debate would already take us out of the quasi-objective social mediation in which the notion of risk is naturalized for the purpose of capture.

The causes of the financial crisis, reread through the framework of capture, reveal that political challenges to finance should focus neither on the system as a whole nor on individual bad actors, but rather on risk itself. Risk is the linchpin that allows financial capture in the form of arbitrage to take place. The system of abstract domination organized by risk channels our everyday practices into risky borrowing and investing to facilitate arbitrage. We should ask what finance and everyday life would look like if we were not condemned to risk and what it would take to get us there.

A Politics of Risk

In Marx's labor theory of value, the commodity is a special figure. It mystifies—fetishizes—the "social relation between men themselves" as if it were a "relation between things" (Marx 2003, 77). The commodity is the thing that carries value to its culmination. But perhaps most importantly of all, there is one commodity that is more special than the rest, the commodity that is actualized when men and women are compelled to sell the only thing that remains to them after the process of primitive accumulation: labor power. Just as wood becomes a chair in the factory, productive activity becomes labor power under the conditions of capitalism. Labor power is an abstract category, the keystone of a metaphysics, and yet it is materialized through the process of production and objectified as the very basis of capitalism. In Postone's (1993) hands, however, labor power is not just the organizing principle of value creation. It is the social mediation to which we are condemned in capitalism. Postone's framing is normative: labor should not be celebrated; it is the object of politics.

In financial capitalism, risk is that object. Our credit scores are not rational reflections of reality; they are lodestones around our necks. And, likewise, risk is in many ways the material basis of all financial activity; risk measurements are used to set the prices at which things trade. This is not an exercise in pure imagination. Risk measurements may be arbitrary, but they create very real social relations and outcomes. Yet financial risk is also a metaphysics, an abstract category that transforms a ubiquitous part of human existence—uncertainty—into the basis of value. In this role, it fetishizes the relations between us, where everyday investments and everyday borrowing produce the circuits of financial value on which excesses are calculated and captured through arbitrage.[1]

Marieke de Goede (2005) argues in *Virtue, Fortune, and Faith* that "risk management combines the political legitimacy of speculation (providing security) with opportunities for unprecedented profit" even while there is "some evidence . . . that complex risk modeling increases overall risk in international financial practices" (141, 142). I have argued that the supposed certainty provided by risk measurements has been shown to be illusory time and time again. Financial crashes and crises are surprises to most. Those who see them coming—or more likely take a chance that they are coming and turn out to be right ex post facto—get their own feature films (*The Big Short* 2015). So if risk measurements purport to provide a window onto the uncertain future, but do a very bad job at it, we are left with two possibilities. In the first, financial professionals are able to more or less accurately measure risk, and risk and return are naturally correlated, leading to right prices that just happen to provide billions of dollars in profit to arbitrageurs who are doing the public service of making markets efficient, at least some of the time. Crises are due to unfortunate errors or inefficiencies, not inadequacies in risk measurement. When they happen, we should—and usually do—get back to business as usual as quickly as possible and by whatever means necessary.

A second possibility is that risk is a construction and abstraction that cannot properly measure the probability of uncertain future events. Instead, financial capitalism, in the service of promoting capture through arbitrage, constructs a system that mystifies radical uncertainty by suggesting that those times when risk measurements are accidentally correct are the result of right risk measurement and the times where risk measurements are just as accidentally incorrect are the result of inefficiencies and perverse incentives. This mystification is made possible by the acceptance of the imaginary universe of economic models and free market ideology (Kwak 2017). In this interpretation, risk is not something we measure to ensure the safety of financial markets, it is something we construct to ensure the profitability of finance for some and not others.

The point of this book is not only to foreground and redefine arbitrage and risk but also to ask how we might challenge the fetish of risk, or at the very least, protect ourselves from the most pernicious effects of the system. I have tried to explain the system of financial value capture, but more than understanding is needed. We are living not only under the abstract domination of race and labor, to which ongoing political action is continuously directed, but also under the abstract domination of risk. We must also find ways to challenge the notion that risk is measurable and that risk and return are correlated and the consequences that the acceptance of these axioms produces. Therefore, in this conclusion, I present some ways that we might direct political action to deconstructing the naturalness of those relations between us that are currently fetishized as relations between risk calculations, and therefore transform the balance of power within financial capitalism. Each of the proposals described below is inevitably half-baked, as all untested ideas must be. Yet I cannot in good conscience offer one more book about financialized capitalism that ends with platitudes about "taking it to the streets." Other futures are possible, but they must begin somewhere. My hope is that these proposals can be generative of new and better political strategies, even if they only show us paths we decide we should not take.[2]

What's in a Price?

Consumer credit in the United States today is a risk-stratified product where prices—that is, interest rates—are set in direct correlation to the credit score and profile of the borrower. This logic is internal to the system of abstract domination in which the axiom of risk and return serves as a base principle. Risk-based pricing emerges out of the union of the axioms of risk and return and risk measurement and the accepted economic notion that price is a natural fact. It is worth pausing on this assumption about prices in order to think about ways to challenge the logic of risk-based pricing.

Economics, like other reductionist social sciences, has historically been concerned with circumscribing the complex contexts that produce phenomena like price in order to make judgments and predictions about them. Classical political economists struggled over the determination of the value or the true price of commodities, alternately citing labor or costs of production as its sole determinant. Adam Smith suggested that labor determined natural prices in primitive societies, while costs of production determined them in advanced society. David Ricardo and Karl Marx held more steadfastly to a labor theory of value. J. S. Mills advocated the cost of production value theory (Colander and Landreth 2001).

The introduction of the concepts of marginal utility and equilibrium by writers in the nineteenth century shifted the ground of classical value theory, redefining natural prices as equilibrium prices determined by supply and demand (Colander and Landreth 2001). This neoclassical price theory viewed supply and demand each as the inevitable result of assumed natural human strivings toward the rational maximization of utility. Utility was conceived as satisfaction, such that demand was determined by the utility received from preferred commodities and supply was determined by the utility received from profit (Wolff and Resnick 1987; Besanko and Braeutigam 2008). Right prices were thus produced by the interplay of supply and demand, each determined by subjective but reliably consistent human nature.

But prices are not, like many things assumed to be the province of the dismal science, reducible to natural origins. They are complex contextual and cultural productions. The best mechanism to understand their formation is not supply and demand, but mattering maps. According to Lawrence Grossberg (1992), "mattering maps define different forms, quantities and places of energy" (82); they are a way of understanding affect and "people's investments in and into the world" (82). Mattering maps designate the significance of things and how those things are arranged in relation to one another. Prices are the result of the contextual process of producing mattering maps. They are born not only out of the tension between supply and demand, but between myriad ways of valuing and the values that people attach to things. They are also a result of power and structural conditions. Pharmaceutical pricing is a prime example. Epinephrine auto-injectors are expensive. And they are undoubtedly highly valued. But they are highly valued because the survival of children with allergies is highly valued in society. In the apparatus of capture of industrial capitalism in which profit from production is the highest goal, epinephrine auto-injectors should be priced as highly as they possibly can be without reducing demand. And demand for EpiPens is inelastic—people need them to survive. But it is not just high demand that allows EpiPens to be priced at $300 per dose.

The structure of healthcare in the United States also conspires to promote high drug prices. Unlike most other developed countries—who see lifesaving pharmaceuticals as public utilities—the United States does not regulate drug prices.[3] For instance, at its highest price, the EpiPen cost nearly ten times more in the United States than in the UK.[4] Despite outrage over the cost, the government did not intervene to reduce prices.[5] Instead, a generic alternative was introduced, ostensibly raising supply, but barely changing the price.[6] That's because the price of the drug is not set only by supply and demand, but by a much more complex intersection of shared values and structures of power.

Prices are the result of calculations built on the mattering maps of particular contexts or "regimes of value" (Appadurai 1986). What something is worth, what someone is willing to pay for something, is determined not by a single preference, but by the intersection of cultures of valuation, structural conditions, and power relations. Prices are, therefore, never fixed by the magical machinations of supply and demand and are cultural rather than natural. This idea is not lost on corporations and business consultants. A group of consultants and a professor of public management authored the book *Contextual Pricing*, in which they offer tools for taking advantage of context. They explain: "Success comes from understanding context. This idea has been leveraged with great results by some leading companies. The Coca-Cola Company, for instance, includes *temperature* at the point of sale in its pricing context. An ice-cold cola commands a better price in the middle of summer on a hot beach than during a snowstorm in the Arctic! Being able to adjust prices to the immediate context of the buying occasion is how Coke has moved to monetize contextual insights" (Docters et al. 2012, 2). While mainstream economists might rationalize these insights as simply techniques for better understanding supply and demand, *Contextual Pricing* actually acknowledges the broader cultural determination of prices, and the inadequacy of marginal utility models.

Understanding the contextual basis of pricing reveals that the axiom of risk and return is not a statement of natural law, but a form of social domination. It directs flows of value toward defining prices according to the logic of risk and return for the purposes of capture. It enables lenders to charge high prices—unnecessarily high, according to the nonprofit lender Self Help Credit Union—that produce the spread for arbitrage capture ("Predatory Lending Practices" 2001). It also disproportionately harms Black borrowers because credit scores concentrate and elide the historical harms of racism and segregation, and facilitate "predatory inclusion" (K. Taylor 2019). But things could be otherwise, particularly in regard to the price of consumer credit. Under risk-based pricing, those who can least afford to pay high interest rates must, while the wealthy pay the lowest or even zero interest. Since the ascendance of risk-based pricing at the end of the 1970s and the introduction of subprime lending in the 1990s, wealth inequality has unsurprisingly widened along multiple vectors, especially race (Dymski et al. 2013).

A politics of risk therefore might involve proposals to reject risk-based pricing itself. If regulation or subsidies were extended to borrowers with low credit scores, the impact on wealth inequality would likely be large. To my knowledge, no one has proposed any policy directed at this outcome. But one could be constructed as an amendment to the Fair Credit Reporting Act or Equal Credit Opportunity Act. If lenders were required to lend to borrowers with low credit scores at the same rates they do to higher rated borrowers, they would claim that lending would become unprofitable, but it remains to be seen whether that would actually be the case. In states that enact payday lending laws capping interest rates, some lenders leave, but many stay, lending at the lower rates (Holmes 2019). The main challenge to enacting such a policy would be to overcome the billions of dollars of lobbying that would be directed against it. Recent history does not bode well for such an effort.

An alternative would be to level the interest rate playing field with subsidies rather than regulation. Enormous government subsidies are routinely given to wealthy individuals and corporations. Wealthy Americans enjoy tax breaks and loopholes as well as low interest rate loans from big lenders. Corporations enjoy a generous system of welfare as well. What's more, the government already intervenes to provide lower interest rates to borrowers with uncertain or low credit scores for the purposes of higher education and, in some cases, homeownership. Interest rate subsidies for other forms of credit like auto loans and credit cards would significantly advantage low-income borrowers. Of course, it would also cost a great deal of taxpayer money. But since the dissolution of the Fordist Compromise, the U.S. government has been more willing to spend taxpayer money than to reign in corporate power. Risk-based pricing is a neglected area in which government regulation or subsidy could create enormous societal benefit.

Measure This

Hand in hand with risk-based pricing, the credit score should also be an object of political scrutiny and action. Outright rejection of the credit score as a criterion for lending and other financial decisions is one option, although Mark Kear (2013) warns that proposing a fully inclusive "financial citizenship" comes with dangers to the economy as a whole (if lenders experience more losses as a result) and that financial institutions could become more powerful regulators of everyday life if more people are included into circuits of consumer credit lending. Alternatively, a politics of risk might meaningfully engage the way in which the credit score is calculated.

Since the inception of statistical credit scoring in the 1960s, lenders have exchanged outright discrimination for mathematical proxies. Josh Lauer explains that variables such as length of time at one's current home or job, or owning a telephone were most predictive of loan default in the middle of the twentieth century. In other words, "stability became a rough proxy for character" (2017, 206). But character is an intrinsic property of an individual, and stability in the United States of the 1960s versus today is at best correlated with and at worst determined by the identity characteristics of gender, race, class, ability, and more due to structural inequalities. The Equal Credit Opportunity Act (ECOA) of 1974/1976 attempted to protect women and later minorities from credit discrimination. But even with the passage of the law, which turned computerized credit scoring systems into "[tools] of legal compliance," "statistical credit scoring could not end discrimination by excluding superficial personal characteristics because gender and racial inequalities were woven directly into the fabric of American society" (240, 238). Through risk-based pricing, these inequalities—now rationalized in statistical credit scores—have become self-reinforcing, stratified financial pressures. The poor and disadvantaged must pay more for credit, making them less likely to use that credit as leverage to get ahead—as businesses do—and more likely to serve as fodder for financial capture. If risk-based pricing cannot be outlawed or ameliorated, then statistical credit discrimination and the negative feedback loop it creates for those with low credit scores could be addressed.

The main barrier to challenging credit discrimination is the legal treatment of credit surveillance and scoring under the ECOA. The act has traditionally been interpreted as a prohibition against "disparate treatment" of protected minorities outlined in its language. Under this standard, discrimination is proven by "statements revealing that a lender explicitly considered prohibited factors (overt evidence) or by differences in treatment that are not fully explained by legitimate nondiscriminatory factors (comparative evidence)" ("Fair Lending" 2015). The prime example of disparate treatment is redlining of minority neighborhoods by banks who then refuse to lend to buyers within that territory. But as Keeanga-Yamahtta Taylor (2019) explains, since the Nixon administration, overt "race talk" has been avoided in policy, and court precedent has subsequently established that, in the absence of such talk, racial discrimination cannot be proven nor, therefore, remedied (20, 243). Since differential treatment of borrowers is now couched in the neutral logic of risk-based pricing, which is accepted as a fair standard for pricing consumer debt, disparate treatment cannot function as a legal standard for remedying the very effects of that risk-based pricing on disadvantaged borrowers.

Borrowers have, however, sued under the ECOA using another standard: disparate impact. Under disparate impact, the act would prohibit any "policy or practice [that] disproportionately excludes or burdens certain persons on a prohibited basis" (W. Taylor 2018). However, according to the Federal Deposit Insurance Corporation, "when an Agency finds that a lender's policy or practice has a disparate impact; the next step is to seek to determine whether the policy or practice is justified by 'business necessity'" ("Fair Lending" 2015). Since profiting from lending operations is certainly a business necessity for lenders, the disparate impact standard has been historically difficult to meet (W. Taylor 2018). What's more, class is not a protected category under the ECOA, so even if disparate impact were explicitly sanctioned by Congress or the Supreme Court, it could not be applied to one group that is very likely to receive and be negatively impacted by high interest rates—the poor.

Law professor Winnie Taylor (2018) has advocated for Congress or the Supreme Court to officially sanction the disparate impact standard as applicable to ECOA. Additionally, income and wealth status should be included in the list of protected categories under the law. The extent of credit surveillance today is enormous. Even if lenders argue that excluding income and wealth from credit scoring would lead to higher defaults and lower profits, they could still use the extensive data and modeling at their disposal to try to predict good credit risks. Similarly, other proposals that attempt to challenge the negative effects of risk-based credit scoring and pricing must be developed and pursued.

One such proposal was been made by Republican Senator Tim Scott of South Carolina and Democratic Senator Mark Warner of Virginia. The "Credit Score Competition Act" would require that the government-sponsored enterprises Fannie Mae and Freddie Mac purchase mortgages that were made not simply on the basis of borrowers' credit scores, but also incorporating "rent, utility, and cell phone bill payments" (Scott 2017). The idea is that incorporating such other measures would allow access to homeownership for previously discriminated against populations. Scott said: "There are millions of Americans who pay their rent, utilities, or cell phone bills on time, yet aren't considered 'credit-worthy' under federal housing finance standards because they lack access to traditional lines of credit, such as auto or student loans. These 'credit invisible' Americans are disproportionately young, new Americans or people of color" (Scott 2017). The Credit Score Competition Act therefore seemed to be aimed at unraveling some of the effects of the union of racial and financial apparatuses of capture in contemporary society. The act passed in 2018, but the version of the rule put into place simply allows Fannie Mae and Freddie Mae to use alternative credit scoring models, none of which require such payments to be considered.[7] Policies that actually incorporate other proxies of financial responsibility could challenge the abstract domination of risk under financial capitalism, but only if they include a provision—like including income and wealth as categories in the ECOA—for preventing risk-based stratification of interest rates for those newly included via such changes in credit scoring.

Strike Risk

In the aftermath of the financial crisis, the Occupy Wall Street (OWS) movement attempted to challenge the dominance of the financial system using a class framework (the 99 percent vs. the 1 percent). One of the outgrowths of OWS was the Strike Debt movement—"a decentralized network of debt resisters, including activists, artists, and organizers" aiming to challenge the system in which people must "go into debt for the basic things in life" ("Strike Debt!"). The problem with the notion of striking or failing to pay debt is that debtors' strike activity directly disadvantages them individually within the system of abstract domination of risk in financial capitalism. Dick Bryan and Michael Rafferty put it this way: Refusing to pay one's debts "would be a politically brave act for the individuals who participate, for they damage their personal credit scores. But this denial does not constitute a collective politics. . . . There needs to be an alternative political response, in which political action is innately collective" (2018, 188).

In their book *Risking Together*, Bryan and Rafferty offer a novel twist on the argument that corporations and governments have been engaged in "risk shifting" in recent decades (Gosselin 2008; Hacker 2006; Standing 2011). They acknowledge that stable full-time work has given way, at least in part, to a precarious gig economy, and that retirement income and other welfare provisions once provided by the state and corporations are now being imposed on individuals. However, they reframe this development not only as a cost-saving tactic but as the result and bedrock of financialization. Households absorb risk by enduring precarious work, being responsible for their own retirement savings (even if that savings is—as it is in Australia—compulsory), and being locked into ever more contracts for the management of risk (insurance) and the provision of everyday life (mortgages, other loans, utilities, memberships, etc.) (166).

This latter development, which they term "contractualism" (31), is the centerpiece of their argument, for they see these contracts not only as engendering risk for households, who must find a way to meet their obligations even when their income is uncertain, but also as a potential political lever because they are the basis of financial profit through securitization. By securitizing debt and other household contracts into financial securities for investors, "finance turns each household into parts of a virtual factory of financial asset production" (106). These assets are safer than traditional financial securities precisely because their underlying value is based not in corporate profits but on the everyday survival of households. Whereas a corporation might default on its bonds if this strategy is ultimately best for its managers or shareholders, households will go to any lengths necessary not to default on their mortgages or have their electricity cut. Bryan and Rafferty thus amend the "risk shifting" argument to show that households are not only risk sinks for corporations and governments; they are also, in that very role as risk sinks, offering new forms of financial profit to traders and investors.

It is in the context of this argument that Bryan and Rafferty offer an alternative to the Strike Debt approach to challenging the worst effects of finance. They propose the notion of "household unions" (2018, 183) as a new collectivity that can enact change. They suggest that households should remit their contractual payments not directly to the services who administer them, but rather to a union that could threaten to "stop repaying in strategic ways" (189). A household strike would constitute a significant "threat to asset values" backed by those payments, a claim they support by referencing the devastation that resulted from the relatively circumscribed but unexpected levels of default that precipitated the 2007–9 financial crisis (190). Rather than a nation of individual payers whose payments are collected together to form the basis of securitizations for profit—a situation very similar to individual workers being gathered together in the physical factory to produce surplus value—household unions would collect individual payments into an aggregate that could be levered to secure "acceptable and stable standards of living for all" (187).

Bryan and Rafferty's proposal has the advantage of not relying on governments to enact new laws or policies that run counter to the interests of banks and other lenders or financial firms. The regulatory capture of the U.S. government by corporate interests is so thorough and entrenched that it strains credulity to imagine that it would play a large role in unraveling the abstract domination of risk that benefits financial firms. Bryan and Rafferty (2018) acknowledge that "there may and probably will be contractual penalties for participants" in a risk strike (190). But as inequality grows, many are living with the penalties of the abstract domination of risk and financial capture already.

The proposals outlined in this conclusion undoubtedly leave much to be desired. Their unintended consequences and shortcomings deserve scrutiny. But the dynamics of financial value capture and risk axioms do as well. The apparatus of financial capture still operates with relative political immunity in a time when struggles for racial justice and higher wages are experiencing high participation and even limited victories in the United States (Grawert and Lau 2019; Schuhrke 2019). The last line of *Inside Job* is not wrong. Some things *are* worth fighting for. My hope is that this book makes clear that we can only win the fight by operating on the battleground of risk.

Introduction: Into the Lions' Den

1. Several of my professors expressed interest in my topic and directed me to resources I used for this book. I was even hired as a teaching assistant for one term by one of my particularly generous professors. I have nothing but praise and gratitude for all the people I came into contact with during my year and a half expedition at the business school.

2. For example, "An arbitrage opportunity arises when an investor can earn riskless profits without making a net investment" (Bodie et al. 2009, 325). Also, "'True' arbitrage is both riskless and self-financing" (Billingsley 2006, 2).

3. "Arbitrage Business: The Stock Exchange Making an Effort to Lessen Its Volume," *New York Times*, September 20, 1892, 9, https://www.nytimes.com/1892/09/20/archives/arbitrage-business-the-stock-exchange-making-an-effort-to-lessen.html.

4. Richard Croft, "Arbitrage Growing in Popularity," *Globe and Mail* (Toronto), September 13, 1986, B2.

5. Elizabeth Rigby, "Running Arbitrage with Attitude," *Financial Times* (London), June 16, 2003, 2.

Chapter 1: Capitalism as Capture

1. Richard Wolff and Stephen Resnick explain the difference between productive and unproductive labor with regard to management: "The productive capitalist directs me to supervise productive laborers, to make sure they perform the maximum possible surplus labor. In this case I do unproductive labor since my labor power is not a direct part of the production of capitalist commodities"(1987, 166). In addition to managing, Wolff and Resnick classify merchanting, renting land, and moneylending as unproductive labor, that is, labor that does not create value, even though it indirectly aids in the production and appropriation of surplus value. Lending at interest is specifically categorized by Wolff and Resnick as an unproductive, "nonclass" process in which "no labor or surplus labor is

done, no new commodities are created" (165). Harry Braverman argues that unproductive labor is that which relates to the realization of surplus value, through the "distribution, storage, packaging, transportation, display, etc." of commodities, or the appropriation of surplus value through "the use of capital simply for purposes of credit, speculation, etc." (1998, 286). Braverman argues that, while realization and appropriation "engage . . . enormous masses of labor," this labor "does not enlarge the value or surplus value available to society or to the capitalist class by one iota" (287).

2. David Harvey explains that all paper claims, including credit money, are "characterized as *fictitious value*" even if they reduce the time and costs of circulation by transforming fixed into circulating capital (1982, 269).

3. "The credit system, which has its focal point in the allegedly national banks and the big money-lenders and usurers that surround them, is one enormous centralization and gives to this class of parasites a fabulous power not only to decimate the industrial capitalists periodically but also to interfere in actual production in the most dangerous manner" (Marx 1991, 678–79).

4. Costas Lapavitsas describes the activities of finance as "financial expropriation," the process of "extracting financial profit directly out of the personal income of workers and others," that has taken place since the 1970s due to "mediocre and precarious growth" in "real accumulation" (2009, 114, 115, 126). Since profits to real production have stagnated, financial expropriation has allowed continued profitability by accessing workers' income in other ways: "The increasing 'financialisation' of individual worker-income is clear, in terms both of liabilities (mostly borrowing for housing) and assets (mostly pensions and insurance)" (129). Yet Lapavitsas is clear that financial expropriation does not involve the production of surplus value. That is, in the last instance, finance is again parasitical, only in this case it leeches value off of workers directly, as in usury, instead of appropriating a share of the surplus value created in production as interest or dividends (131).

5. Ivan Ascher (2016) argues that prediction—determining the probabilities of default— is the hidden abode of finance. Much of his book *Portfolio Society* maps the very same processes I do in this book. However, he foregrounds hedging and prediction rather than arbitrage and risk as defining processes in financial capitalism. Additionally, whereas I consider risk to be the principle of abstract domination in finance, he describes it as a commodity. I consider these differences to be largely ones of framing, and consider *Portfolio Society* as a sister text to this one.

6. *Kirtsaeng v. John Wiley and Sons, Inc.*, 568 U.S. 519 (2013). Thanks to Ian Murphy for bringing this example to my attention.

7. *Kirtsaeng v. John Wiley and Sons, Inc.*, 568 U.S. 519 (2013).

8. Marx considered slaves to be a form of capital (2003, 253).

9. Other colonial contexts may also fit into the capture framework as well. Robert Nichols (2018) suggests that the process of dispossession in which indigenous lands are appropriated by colonizers constitutes those lands as property per se. He argues that "colonization

entails the large-scale transfer of land that simultaneously recodes the object of exchange in question such that it appears retrospectively to be a form of theft in the ordinary sense. It is thus not (only) about the transfer of property, but the transformation into property" (14). The "recursive logic" of the colonial system "produces what it presupposes (namely, property)" (20, 15). Nichols's argument aligns with Deleuze and Guattari's definition of capture as a process in which comparison constitutes the very stock of value, suggesting that the capture of indigenous lands is another form of capture.

10. John Preston (2010) has advanced a similar argument in which he distinguishes concrete racial domination and abstract racial domination. In his formulation, "abstract racial domination [is] a unique form of racial oppression in capitalism . . . that aside from concrete racial domination (what critical race theorists call 'white supremacy'), capitalism produces an insidious form of abstract racial domination (or domination by race as capital)" (116). For Preston, "concrete racial domination is, then, a system of oppression that denies humanity to people of colour" and abstract racial domination involves the use of whiteness as capital (116). My argument is different. I do not suggest that race is (solely) a capital in itself, but rather that race is the principle which, under racial capitalism, creates "differential value" through "the production of recognized differences that result in distinct kinds of values" (Pulido 2017, 527).

11. The notion of risk evident in the "risk society" literature associated with Ulrich Beck and Anthony Giddens is related to but different from the one that circulates within academic and popular financial discourses. The connotations of the term in the former context revolve around notions of danger, security, and insurance, as well as the governmentality associated with a risk-oriented modernity. In the latter, risk is sanitized into a mathematical measurement of potential variation from some norm (i.e., expected return). This latter notion of financial risk is fundamental to the practice of arbitrage.

12. "Profit arises out of the inherent, absolute unpredictability of things, out of the sheer brute fact that the results of human activity cannot be anticipated and then only in so far as even a probability calculation in regard to them is impossible and meaningless" (Knight 1921, qtd. in Rubenstein 2006, 51).

13. Edward LiPuma and Benjamin Lee (2004) trace a similar "objectification of abstract risk" from Marzowitz to Black and Scholes, and claim that "the final and continuing dimension in the formal objectification of risk has been its quantification through stochastic formulas, such as those invented by Black and Scholes" (147).

14. Examples of this genre abound. One depicts grandparents on a speedboat with their granddaughter ("Fidelity Investments" 2017). Another shows a grumpy child only coming alive when she jumps into the ocean on her tropical vacation ("Northwestern Mutual" 2017). Yet another shows an older couple cleaning elephants' feet on a volunteer safari trip ("Chase Private Client" 2019). All end in the same way, suggesting that all these things can be yours if you pay the right advisor to help you invest in financial securities.

15. Two other popular examples of this narrative can be found in Matt Taibbi's (2010) feature in *Rolling Stone*, entitled "The Great American Bubble Machine," in which he

famously describes Goldman Sachs as "a great vampire squid wrapped around the face of humanity," and Senator Carl Levin's interview with the *New York Times* regarding the official *Financial Crisis Inquiry Report*, in which he states: "The report pulls back the curtain on shoddy, risky, deceptive practices on the part of a lot of major financial institutions. . . . The overwhelming evidence is that those institutions deceived their clients and deceived the public, and they were aided and abetted by deferential regulators and credit rating agencies who had conflicts of interest" (Gretchen Morgenson and Louise Story, "Naming Culprits in the Financial Crisis," *New York Times*, April 13, 2011, http://www.nytimes.com /2011/04/14/business/14crisis.html).

16. Alain Sherter, "In Day of Protests, 'Occupy Wall Street' Faces Police Violence," CBS *News*, November 17, 2011, https://www.cbsnews.com/news/in-day-of-protests-occupy -wall-street-faces-police-violence/.

17. Harvey (2005) and Ascher (2016) make similar arguments.

Chapter 2: Arbitrage in Theory

1. I'm grateful to Ron Becker for numerous stimulating conversations about this book, including the one in which he described the dynamic explained in this chapter as "wish fulfillment."

2. A common finance textbook defines fundamental analysis as "research to predict stock value that focuses on such determinants as earnings and dividends prospects, expectations for future interest rates, and risk evaluation of the firm" (Bodie et al. 2009, G-6).

3. Rubenstein (2006) finds an early example of "arbitrage reasoning" in John Maynard Keynes's 1923 explanation of "normal backwardation" in futures markets, and suggests that the "modern view of John Burr Williams's 1938 present value formula would be that it "follows from no arbitrage" (52, 76). However, Rubenstein quotes Modigliani and Miller as pointing out that the main difference between previous writers and their own argument is that theirs has "the pure arbitrage mechanism underlying our proof" (qtd. in Rubenstein 2006, 123).

4. According to Rubenstein, Modigliani and Miller's scenario should be understood not as arbitrage but as "dominance" because it "does not require that one be sold short against the other to create arbitrage profits" (2006, 124). Nevertheless, the proposition still represents an important starting point for basing financial models on arbitrage logic.

5. Modigliani and Miller (1958) also assumed a "perfect market," with no fees or interest, and perfect equivalence between shares of different firms (268).

6. Donald MacKenzie chronicles the history of exactly this in *An Engine, Not a Camera*, and suggests that it is an important example of economic performativity: "The effects of the use of the Black-Scholes-Merton model in arbitrage thus seem to have formed a direct performative loop between 'theory' and 'reality'" (2006, 166).

7. According to MacKenzie (2006), this is the flagship example of the strongest Barnesian form of performativity he describes in his book.

8. Rubenstein claims that "arbitrage reasoning" was used to price futures in the ancient period (2006, 52).

9. The history of this law is more difficult to trace than that of arbitrage reasoning more generally. It is unclear who first enumerated the law, yet it begins to show up in economics articles shortly after the BSM was published, almost always in quotation marks ("the law of one price") but unattributed to any particular author. See, for example, Branson (1975) and Isard (1977).

10. Bruno J. Navarro, "High-Frequency Trading Benefits Investors: Advocate," CNBC, April 2, 2014, http://www.cnbc.com/2014/04/02/high-frequency-trading-benefits -investors-advocate.html.

11. Tom Joyce, "High-Frequency Trading Provides Essential Liquidity," Wall Street Journal, January 4, 2013, https://www.wsj.com/articles/SB10001424127887323820104578211663170770852.

12. Graham Bowley, "Lone $4.1 Billion Sale Led to 'Flash Crash' in May," New York Times, October 1, 2010, https://www.nytimes.com/2010/10/02/business/02flash.html; Ellen Brown, "Computerized Front Running: Another Goldman-Dominated Fraud," Huffpost, May 25, 2011, https://www.huffpost.com/entry/computerized-front-runnin _b_548148.

13. Thanks to one of my anonymous reviewers for pointing out that referees are called arbitre in French and arbitro in Spanish.

14. Sullivan and Long, Inc. v. Scattered Corp., 47 F.3d 857 C.A.7 (Ill.) (7th Cir. 1995). Thanks to Miami University alumnus and attorney Jeff Patton for bringing this case to my attention.

15. According to James Kwak, Judge Posner was one of several influential American figures (including Gary Becker and George Stigler) who are responsible for applying the logic of Economics 101 (what Kwak calls "economism") to more and more aspects of society, including in Posner's case, legal decisions (2017, 42).

16. Sullivan and Long, Inc. v. Scattered Corp. (1995, 862).

17. This is remarkable since, in the very same speech, Roye also discusses the way that arbitrageurs dilute (reduce long-term returns to) mutual funds for retail investors through market timing. In 2003, the SEC would begin investigating and ultimately fining funds that allowed this kind of arbitrage (Houge and Wellman 2005). But, even during that scandal, arbitrage wasn't vilified. The problem was with the way mutual fund pricing was executed (inefficiently) and rules were needed to prevent that inefficiency from reducing investors' returns.

18. Richard Croft, "Arbitrage Growing in Popularity," Globe and Mail (Toronto), September 13, 1986, B2; Militello 1984; Elizabeth Rigby, "Running Arbitrage with Attitude," Financial Times (London), June 16, 2003, 2.

Chapter 3: Arbitrage IRL

A portion of the research presented in this chapter was adapted for "Introducing a Cultural Approach to Technology in Financial Markets" (Hardin and Rottinghaus 2015).

1. *Oxford Dictionary of Finance and Banking* (2014), s.v. "arbitrage."

2. The only meaningful differentiation that can be made between investing and speculation in this register is in the potential direction of changes in value over time. Investing is undertaken in hopes that the original investment will be returned with an additional profit. Speculation also seeks a profit in the future, but does not necessarily profit from increased returns. For example, one can speculate using futures by entering a futures contract to sell corn at $450 per bushel in one month in hopes that corn will actually trade for $440 at that future time. In that case, buying corn at the prevailing market price, then fulfilling one's contract at $450 a bushel will net a $10 per bushel profit. A decrease in price may still produce a positive speculative return. If the price rises to $460, the speculator will lose $10, making speculation, like investing, an uncertain endeavor. Both investing and time-speculation seek profit from openness to time—from the possibility of change between the present and the future—but speculation may profit from a decrease or increase in value, depending on the strategy used, whereas investing profits only from an increase in value.

3. Scott Patterson, "High-Speed Stock Traders Turn to Laser Beams," *Wall Street Journal*, February 11, 2014, https://www.wsj.com/articles/highspeed-stock-traders-turn-to-laser -beams-1392175358.

4. Inspiration for this term comes from Sarah Sharma's *In the Meantime* (2014).

5. Theoretically, the act of buying goods in one market increases demand and thus may increase price. Similarly, selling goods in another market increases supply and thus may decrease price. In markets where supply and demand have these effects, arbitrage trading will eventually raise the price of cheap goods and lower the price of expensive goods until the disparity of prices (essential to the possibility of arbitrage profit) is erased. This does not always occur, but in many cases it does.

6. Ingham (2004) locates the timing of this development in the sixteenth and seventeenth centuries. Toward the end of the sixteenth century in Holland "changes to the parties involved in a [bill of exchange] contract were written on the back of a bill and this was accepted as an order to pay. . . . The document itself was now deemed to contain all necessary information, and, in effect, signifiers of debt had become depersonalized" (120). The chartering of the Bank of England in 1697 gave the English sovereign a "monopoly to deal in bills of exchange" which were accepted as payment of taxes and became a fully circulating public currency (129).

7. In *In the Meantime*, Sarah Sharma claims that "the explanatory power of speed works to produce differential time and exacerbate structural inequalities experienced at the level of time" (2014, 15). This insight is borne out in the way that network differentials are not always, though sometimes, achieved through speed.

8. This is, of course, not a dynamic unique to arbitrage. Capitalist competition in general involves the race to achieve relative technological advantages. In the case of arbitrage, this race is directed toward the activity of buying and selling securities rather than production, advertising, or consumer surveillance.

9. "Arbitrage Business: The Stock Exchange Making an Effort to Lessen Its Volume," *New York Times*, September 20, 1892, 9, https://www.nytimes.com/1892/09/20/archives/arbitrage-business-the-stock-exchange-making-an-effort-to-lessen.html.

10. A stock index is a calculated value for an aggregated group of stocks, such as the S&P 500 or Dow Jones Industrial Index.

11. Buying and selling five hundred individual stocks would involve transaction costs (commissions, etc.) so high as to completely erode any arbitrage profit (Bodie, Kane, and Marcus 2009, 799). A smaller subset is often used.

12. Bob Pisani, "Man vs. Machine: How Stock Trading Got So Complex," CNBC, September 13, 2010, https://www.cnbc.com/id/38978686.

13. "Arbitrage is the process of buying assets in one market and selling them in another to profit from unjustifiable price differences. 'True' arbitrage is both riskless and self-financing" (Billingsley 2006, 2).

14. Scott McMurray "Here's Another Reason Why," *Wall Street Journal*, January 4, 1985.

15. Jay Palmer, "What Do You Think?—A Nationwide Poll of Reaction to the Crash," *Barron's*, November 9, 1987.

16. Nathaniel Nash, "Task Force Ties Market Collapse to Big Investors' Program Trades," *New York Times*, January 9, 1988, http://www.nytimes.com/1988/01/09/business/task-force-ties-market-collapse-to-big-investors-program-trades.html.

17. Cal Mankowski, "Program Trading Ban Approved by New York Stock Exchange," *Reuters*, February 5, 1988.

18. Anise C. Wallace, "Program Trading Gets More Brutal," *New York Times*, May 1, 1988.

19. Wallace, "Program Trading."

20. Steve Swartz and Kevin G. Salwen, "Five Companies Decide to Halt Index Trades: Securities Firms Won't Use the Program Technique for Their Own Accounts," *Wall Street Journal*, May 11, 1988.

21. Kurt Eichenwald, "Revolt Spreading on Street against Index Arbitrage Use," Market Place, *New York Times*, October 27, 1989.

22. Eichenwald, "Revolt Spreading on Street."

23. Mark Gongloff, "High-Frequency Trading Is Bad for Profits, Including Those of High-Speed Traders: Study," *Huffington Post Business*, June 18, 2013, http://www.huffingtonpost.com/2013/06/18/high-frequency-trading-profits_n_3459497.html.

24. Felix Salmon, "Don't Cry 'for the Little Guy on Wall Street,'" *Reuters*, September 3, 2013, https://www.reuters.com/article/idUS227672226220130902.

25. Gregory Meyer, Nicole Bullock, and Joe Rennison, "How High Frequency Trading Hit a Speed Bump," *Financial Times*, January 1, 2018, https://global.factiva.com/ha/default .aspx#./!?&_suid=1582058766257039922810194966602.

26. Matthew Phillips, "How the Robots Lost: High-Frequency Trading's Rise and Fall," *Bloomberg Business*, June 6, 2013, http://www.bloomberg.com/bw/articles/2013-06-06 /how-the-robots-lost-high-frequency-tradings-rise-and-fall.

27. This claim was swiftly rebutted using the benevolent-efficiency narrative: "And while the system could be abused to engage in front-running of clients, the fact of its existence speaks more to arbitrage across multiple markets for orderly price formation" (Dannhauser 2014).

Chapter 4: The Postonian Turn

1. This is only true for open-end funds. Closed-end funds trade between investors in the market and so the price of shares may be above or below NAV ("Open-End Fund" 2018; "Closed-End Fund" 2018).

2. In the case of shunting described in chapter 3, the equivalence between shares of stock in the same company trading on different exchanges may seem self-evident. In the case of index arbitrage, the equivalence between the index futures and the basket of current stocks used to approximate it is more obviously theory dependent. First of all, the arbitrage is premised on the mathematical relationship between the futures contract and the spot prices specified by the futures pricing formula. The formula specifies the no-arbitrage price of futures based on current stock prices. The formula, and the no-arbitrage pricing theory that underpins it, therefore signals to the arbitrageur when a potential profit is available. The arbitrage is dependent on that theory even if, as behavioral economists have pointed out, it may not always hold true. Second, traders theorize that the particular basket of stocks they purchase or sell in the present to offset their futures contract will "closely mirror" the full index, which in the case of the commonly used S&P 500 contains 500 stocks (Hull 2008, 110). Traders must rely on an assumption of representativeness, often based on regression models of past price comovement, in order to undertake the arbitrage between the futures and the approximate basket of stocks.

3. This occurs for three reasons. First, administrative costs that must be borne by the mutual fund increase with multiple, rapid, short-term trades. Second, managers may not have enough time to invest quick in- and out-flows of cash, such that that money never goes to work earning returns for the fund as a whole. But, most importantly, when arbitrageurs buy the fund at the stale prices, they gain immediate access to returns. They realize the returns when they sell the next day upon the recalculation of the NAV. Part of those returns is cashed out by arbitrageurs, instead of being delivered to long-term investors.

4. In *A Brief History of Neoliberalism*, David Harvey argues that finance constitutes the "real cutting edge" of what he calls "accumulation by dispossession" (2005, 162, 159). Accumulation by dispossession is not a process of appropriating surplus value through the pro-

duction process, but rather "the continuation and proliferation of accumulation practices which Marx had treated of as 'primitive' or 'original' during the rise of capitalism" (159). Costas Lapavitsas gives another term for his rethinking of the role of finance in capitalism: "financial expropriation" (2009, 114). Financial expropriation is "extracting financial profit directly out of the personal income of workers and others" (115). Lapavitsas suggests that contemporary financial expropriation has much in common with precapitalist usury. Neither Harvey nor Lapavitsas call finance exploitation outright, however, because it is not labor, and labor is, for traditional Marxists, the sole source of value.

5. Bryan and Rafferty (2007) suggest—in line with Mann's proposition—that financial derivatives are a new general equivalent, i.e., money.

6. Emmie Martin, "67% of Americans Say They'll Outlive Their Retirement Savings— Here's How Many Have Nothing Saved at All," CNBC, May 14, 2018, https://www.cnbc .com/2018/05/11/how-many-americans-have-no-retirement-savings.html.

7. It might be immediately remarked that the fact that so many are not able to invest disqualifies the analogy between labor and investing. But, of course, many are not able to labor as well, due to disability, infirmity, or social/cultural reasons such as age, caregiving responsibilities, or participation in other activities like education. These contextual conditions do not disrupt the abstract domination function of labor, just like the lack of wealth to invest for some—conditioned by factors like class, gender, and race—does not disqualify the abstract domination of the compulsion to invest for retirement.

Chapter 5: Money Machines

A great deal of the technical detail relayed in the second part of this chapter was clarified by many lengthy conversations with Robert Wosnitzer, a former bond trader turned cultural studies researcher turned business school professor. The argument made herein wouldn't have come together without his gracious assistance.

1. Gary Fields, "States Go to War over Cigarette Smuggling," *Wall Street Journal*, July 20, 2009, https://www.wsj.com/articles/SB124804682785163691.

2. As Benjamin Lee puts it, "In the financial literature, arbitrage is represented as a form of 'negative performativity': the representation of a difference leads to the self-referential cancellation of that difference" (2016, 95).

3. These limits might include storage costs and convenience yields (Hull 2009).

4. The fully amortized mortgage—with equal payments across time—was invented in 1934, but the thirty-year mortgage term wasn't established until 1948. This was also the year Fannie Mae began buying Veterans Administration mortgages (Green and Wachter 2005; Hyman 2011).

5. Prepayment was, however, a significant risk that could reduce the payoff to these securities if mortgage borrowers refinanced their mortgages.

6. Fannie Mae and Freddie Mac differ slightly in the extent of their guarantees, as the Housing Act of 1968 allows the U.S. Treasury to buy Fannie Mae–backed MBS as a "last resort." Freddie Mac enjoys no such provision (Hyman 2011, 232).

7. In the 1980s, banks and other financial firms began to securitize multiple forms of debt, including credit cards, auto loans, and home equity loans. These securitizations are known together as "asset-backed securities" or ABS.

8. Banks and GSEs now also structure tranched instruments on guaranteed loans as well, called "collateralized mortgage obligations" (CMOs) to distinguish them from "pass through" MBS (Hyman 2011, 237).

9. Exact grades differ slightly between the three major credit rating agencies, Fitch Group, Standard and Poor's, and Moody's.

10. Felix Salmon, "A Formula for Disaster," *Wired* 17, no. 3 (March 2009).

11. Jesse Eisinger and Jake Bernstein, "The Magnetar Trade: How One Hedge Fund Helped Keep the Bubble Going," *ProPublica*, April 2, 2010, http://www.propublica.org /article/all-the-magnetar-trade-how-one-hedge-fund-helped-keep-the-housing-bubble.

12. Serena Ng and Carrick Mollenkamp, "A Fund behind Astronomical Losses," *Wall Street Journal*, January 14, 2008, http://www.wsj.com/articles/SB120027155742887331.

Chapter 6: The Emperor's New Clothes

1. This practice is known as regulatory arbitrage because it compares the regulatory treatment of one asset to that of another and in making the exchange frees up regulatory capital for profit-making activities. However, this exchange is not an actual arbitrage trade as it only puts previously static funds into flow rather than capturing new value; but it provided an incentive to banks to securitize their subprime loans and then buy AAA-rated subprime CDOs.

2. Aaron Lucchetti and Serena Ng, "'Ratings Shopping' Lives as Congress Debates a Fix," *Wall Street Journal*, May 24, 2010, http://www.wsj.com/articles/SB10001424052748703315 404575250270972715804.

3. Chappe, Nell, and Semmler similarly point out the "epistemic fallacy" of "the paradigm of quantifiable risk" in their 2013 article (12, 14). They seem to share my interpretation that the notion of risk both underpins financial activity and is not actually quantifiable in the way assumed by financial market participants. However, they attribute allegiance to the paradigm of quantifiable risk to "cognitive failure": "a failure to acknowledge that the future is to a large degree uncertain" (22). I am not arguing—as they do—that finance is skewed by cognitive failure built on the use of "flawed models." In my framework, quantifiable risk is not an ideological principle, false or otherwise, but rather is axiomatic to the functioning of finance at a more basic level. Despite their implicit argument that more accurate models are possible, Chappe, Nell, and Semmler provide evidence of this deeper

role of risk, noting that "the high degree of confidence placed in the concept of risk as a form of indeterminacy that can be controlled and measured with probabilistic models has served as a convenient discourse for legitimizing business decisions" (31). I will drive their point even further: risk measurement occurs at multiple critical nodes within financial circuits because it must for financial capture to occur. Without it, modern finance could not exist, at least in its current form. In the context of the CDO arbitrage, neither borrower credit scores nor CDO credit ratings would be intelligible without this axiom. Without these two inputs, the arbitrage never could have happened.

4. Hyman (2011) notes that the sale of low-quality merchandise at prices so high that repossession is likely, allowing for a new sale and thus recurring profit, is a long-standing practice in ghetto economies.

5. "Bush Aims to Boost Minority Home Ownership," InsidePolitics, CNN.com, June 17, 2002, http://www.cnn.com/2002/ALLPOLITICS/06/17/bush.minority.homes/index .html.

6. "Fannie and Freddie were required to meet affordable housing goals, set annually by the Department of Housing and Urban Development (HUD) in accordance with the Federal Housing Enterprises Financial Safety and Soundness Act of 1992. The purchase of PLS [private-label securitizations] backed by subprime mortgages counted toward meeting these goals because the underlying mortgages tended to be made to less than median income borrowers or were collateralized by properties in 'underserved areas'" (Thomas and Van Order 2010, 4).

7. Jonnelle Marte, "Wells Fargo Steered Blacks and Latinos toward Costlier Mortgages, Philadelphia Lawsuit Alleges," *Los Angeles Times*, May 16, 2017, http://www.latimes.com /business/la-fi-wells-fargo-philadelphia-20170516-story.html.

Conclusion: A Politics of Risk

1. Ivan Ascher (2016) has already made this assertion before me, writing: "I claim that we find a similar fetishism in today's financial markets. These are markets that allow us to take risks together, undoubtedly, but where the distinctly social character of our risk-taking relations appears to us in a most curious form—as relations among the securities them-selves" (28). Where my argument differs from Ascher's is that he sees prediction as the hidden abode of financial capitalism—an argument that may take the existence of risks for granted—while I find the framing of abstract domination more helpful in revealing risk itself as the mystification par excellence of financial capitalism.

2. Thanks to Larry Grossberg for explaining to me that learning which roads are dead ends is just as useful as charting fruitful new territory.

3. Sarah Kliff, "The True Story of America's Sky-High Prescription Drug Prices," *vox*, May 10, 2018, https://www.vox.com/science-and-health/2016/11/30/12945756 /prescription-drug-prices-explained.

4. Toni Clarke, "U.S. Lawmakers Blast Mylan CEO over 'Sickening' EpiPen Price Hikes," *Reuters*, September 21, 2016, https://www.reuters.com/article/us-mylan-nl-epipen-congress/u-s-lawmakers-blast-mylan-ceo-over-sickening-epipen-price-hikes-idUSKCN11R2OG.

5. Stephanie Zimmerman, "Despite Promise by FDA Boss of Lower Cost, New Generic EpiPen Isn't Any Cheaper," *Chicago Sun-Times*, December 1, 2018, https://chicago.suntimes.com/news/epipen-epinepherine-teva-generic-allergy-allergies-consumer-health-costs-fda-drug-prices-scott-gottlieb/.

6. Zimmerman, "Despite Promise."

7. Ben Lane, "FHFA flip-flops, won't blacklist VantageScore as FICO alternative for Fannie and Freddie," *Housing Wire*, August 13, 2019, https://www.housingwire.com/articles/49847-fhfa-flip-flops-wont-blacklist-vantagescore-as-fico-alternative-for-fannie-and-freddie/.

REFERENCES

Acharya, Viral V., Thomas Philippon, Matthew Richardson, and Nouriel Roubini. 2009. "The Financial Crisis of 2007–2009: Causes and Remedies." In *Restoring Financial Stability: How to Repair a Failed System*, edited by Viral V. Acharya and Matthew Richardson 2009, 1–56. Hoboken, NJ: John Wiley and Sons.

Acharya, Viral V., and Matthew Richardson, eds. 2009. *Restoring Financial Stability: How to Repair a Failed System*. Hoboken, NJ: John Wiley and Sons.

Allon, Fiona. 2010. "Speculating on Everyday Life: The Cultural Economy of the Quotidian." *Journal of Communication Inquiry* 34, no. 4: 366–81.

Allon, Fiona, and Guy Redden. 2012. "The Global Financial Crisis and the Culture of Continual Growth." *Journal of Cultural Economy* 5, no. 4: 375–90.

Amoore, Louise. 2013. *The Politics of Possibility: Risk and Security beyond Probability*. Durham, NC: Duke University Press.

Anthony, Sebastian. 2014. "New Laser Network between NYSE and NASDAQ Will Allow High-Frequency Traders to Make Even More Money." ExtremeTech.com. February 14. http://www.extremetech.com/extreme/176551-new-laser-network-between-nyse-and-nasdaq-will-allow-high-frequency-traders-to-make-even-more-money.

Appadurai, Arjun. 1986. "Introduction: Commodities and the Politics of Value." In *The Social Life of Things: Commodities in Cultural Perspective*, edited by Arjun Appadurai, 3–63. Cambridge: Cambridge University Press.

Ascher, Ivan. 2016. *Portfolio Society: On the Capitalist Mode of Prediction*. New York: Zone Books.

Ashcraft, Adam B., and Til Schuermann. 2008. "Understanding the Securitization of Subprime Mortgage Credit." *Federal Reserve Bank of New York Staff Reports* 318. New York.

Baradaran, Mehrsa. 2017. *The Color of Money: Black Banks and the Racial Wealth Gap*. Cambridge, MA: Belknap Press of Harvard University Press.

Baucom, Ian. 2005. *Specters of the Atlantic: Finance Capital, Slavery, and the Philosophy of History*. Durham, NC: Duke University Press.

Benmelech, Efraim, and Jennifer Dlugosz. 2009. "The Alchemy of CDO Credit Ratings." *Journal of Monetary Economics* 56, no. 2: 617–34.

Bernstein, Peter L. 1998. *Against the Gods: The Remarkable Story of Risk*. Hoboken, NJ: John Wiley and Sons.

Besanko, David, and Ronald Braeutigam. 2008. *Microeconomics*. 3rd ed. Hoboken, NJ: John Wiley and Sons.

Beunza, Daniel, Ian Hardie, and Donald MacKenzie. 2006. "A Price Is a Social Thing: Towards a Material Sociology of Arbitrage." *Organization Studies* 27, no. 5: 722–41.

Beunza, Daniel, and David Stark. 2004. "Tools of the Trade: The Socio-Technology of Arbitrage in a Wall Street Trading Room." *Industrial and Corporate Change* 13, no. 2: 369–400.

The Big Short. 2015. Directed by Adam McKay. Los Angeles: Paramount Pictures. DVD.

Billingsley, Randall S. 2006. *Understanding Arbitrage: An Intuitive Approach to Investment Analysis*. Upper Saddle River, NJ: Wharton School Publications.

Bishop-Henchman, Joseph, and Scott Drenkard. 2014. "Cigarette Taxes and Cigarette Smuggling by State." TaxFoundation.org. March 19. https://taxfoundation.org/cigarette-taxes-and-cigarette-smuggling-state.

Black, Fischer, and Myron Scholes. 1973. "The Pricing of Options and Corporate Liabilities." *Journal of Political Economy* 81, no. 3: 637–54.

Bodie, Zvi, Alex Kane, and Alan J. Marcus. 2009. *Investments*. 8th ed. New York: McGraw-Hill.

Branson, William H. 1975. "Monetarist and Keynesian Models of the Transmission of Inflation." *American Economic Review* 65, no. 2: 115–19.

Braverman, Harry. 1998. *Labor and Monopoly Capital: The Degradation of Work in the Twentieth Century*. New York: Monthly Review Press.

Bryan, Dick, and Michael Rafferty. 2007. "Financial Derivatives and the Theory of Money." *Economy and Society* 36, no. 1: 134–58.

Bryan, Dick, and Michael Rafferty. 2013. "Fundamental Value: A Category in Transformation." *Economy and Society* 42, no. 1: 130–53.

Bryan, Dick, and Michael Rafferty. 2018. *Risking Together: How Finance Is Dominating Everyday Life in Australia*. Sydney: Sydney University Press.

Bureau of Labor Statistics. 2012. "Table 2. Retirement Benefits: Access, Participation, and Takeup Rates, Private Industry Workers." *National Compensation Survey*. www.bls.gov/ncs/ebs/benefits/2012/ownership/private/table02a.pdf.

Butrica, Barbara A., Howard M. Iams, Karen E. Smith, and Erik J. Toder. 2007. "The Disappearing Defined Benefit Pension and Its Potential Impact on the Retirement Incomes of Baby Boomers." *Social Security Bulletin* 69, no. 3. https://www.ssa.gov/policy/docs/ssb/v69n3/v69n3p1.html.

Calder, Lendol. 1999. *Financing the American Dream: A Cultural History of Consumer Credit*. Princeton, NJ: Princeton University Press.

Calhoun, Michael. 2018. "Lessons from the Financial Crisis: The Central Importance of a Sustainable, Affordable and Inclusive Housing Market." Brookings Institution. September 5. https://www.brookings.edu/research/lessons-from-the-financial-crisis-the-central-importance-of-a-sustainable-affordable-and-inclusive-housing-market/.

Carey, James W. 1992. *Communication as Culture: Essays on Media and Society*. New York: Routledge.

Chandrashekaran, Vinod. 1998. "October's Market Demons: The '87 Stock Market Crash and Likelihood of a Recurrence." *Risk and Rewards Newsletter*, Society of Actuaries 31.

Chappe, Raphaële, Edward Nell, and Willi Semmler. 2013. "The Financial Crisis of 2008 as Cognitive Failure: An Overview of Risk over Uncertainty." *Berkeley Journal of Sociology* 57:9–39.

"Chase Private Client TV Commercial, 'Plan Yourself Free.'" 2019. iSpot.tv. https://www.ispot.tv/ad/I1iO/chase-private-client-plan-yourself-free.

Chen, Natasha, Arturo Cifuentes, Manish Desai, and Anik Ray. 2005. "The Young and the Restless: Correlation Drama at the Big Three Rating Agencies." *Wachovia Securities*, New York, February 22.

"Closed-End Fund." 2018. Investopedia.com. Reviewed by James Chen. February 7. https://www.investopedia.com/terms/c/closed-endinvestment.asp.

Colander, David C., and Harry Landreth. 2001. *History of Economic Thought.* New York: Cengage Learning.

The Complex Story of American Debt: Liabilities in Family Balance Sheets. 2015. Pew Charitable Trusts. July. https://www.pewtrusts.org/-/media/assets/2015/07/reach-of-debt-report_artfinal.pdf?la=en&hash=168FE15FB45F7BEFF758E0D0F5D46786D4629E05.

"Consumer Price Indexes." Federal Reserve Bank of St. Louis. Accessed October 30, 2020. http://fred.stlouisfed.org/categories/9.

Cooper, Melinda. 2017. *Family Values: Between Neoliberalism and the New Social Conservatism.* New York: Zone Books.

Covey, David, Michael Koss, Akhil Mago, Jasraj Vaidya, Brian Zola, Rahul Sabarwal, Dick Kazarian, Dan Mingelgrin, Stefano Risa, Vivien Huang, Omar Brav, and Gaetan Ciampini. 2006. "ABS CDOs—A Primer." *Lehman Brothers Fixed Income: U.S. Securitized Products Research.*

"Credit Suisse Pleads Guilty to Tax Crime Charges. But Is Anyone Going to Jail?" 2014. Audio recording, produced by Christopher Woolf. *PRI's The World.* May 20, 2014. http://www.pri.org/stories/2014-05-20/credit-suisse-pleads-guilty-tax-crime-charges-anyone-going-jail.

Curran, Rob. 2013. "Make $377,000 Trading Apple in One Day." Term Sheet. *Fortune,* August 30, 2013. http://fortune.com/2013/08/30/make-377000-trading-apple-in-one-day/.

Dannhauser, Bob. 2014. "Debating Michael Lewis's 'Flash Boys': High-Frequency Trading Not All Bad." Market Integrity Insights. *CFA Institute,* April 7, 2014. https://blogs.cfainstitute.org/marketintegrity/2014/04/07/debating-michael-lewis-flash-boys-high-frequency-trading-not-all-bad/.

de Goede, Marieke. 2005. *Virtue, Fortune and Faith: A Genealogy of Finance.* Minneapolis: University of Minnesota Press.

Deleuze, Gilles, and Félix Guattari. 2007. *A Thousand Plateaus: Capitalism and Schizophrenia.* Translated by Brian Massumi. Minneapolis: University of Minnesota Press.

De Long, J. Bradford, Andrei Shleifer, Lawrence H. Summers, and Robert J. Waldmann. 1990. "Noise Trader Risk in Financial Markets." *Journal of Political Economy* 98, no. 4: 703–38.

Derman, Emanuel. 2013. "Lecture 1: The Principles of Valuation." Handout, Columbia University, New York.

DeSilver, Drew. 2018. "For Most U.S. Workers, Real Wages Have Barely Budged in Decades." Pew Research Center. August 7, 2018. http://www.pewresearch.org/fact-tank /2018/08/07/for-most-us-workers-real-wages-have-barely-budged-for-decades/.

Docters, Robert, Michael Barzelay, John G. Hanson, and Cecilia Nguyen. 2012. *Contextual Pricing: The Death of List Price and the New Market Reality.* New York: McGraw-Hill.

Duménil, Gérard, and Dominique Lévy. 2011. *The Crisis of Neoliberalism.* Cambridge, MA: Harvard University Press.

Dwyer, Rachel. 2018. "Credit, Debt, and Inequality." *Annual Review of Sociology* 44, no. 1: 237–61.

Dymski, Gary, Jesus Hernandez, and Lisa Mohanty. 2013. "Race, Gender, Power, and the US Subprime Mortgage and Foreclosure Crisis: A Meso Analysis." *Feminist Economics* 19, no. 3: 124–51.

Einzig, Paul. 1970. *The History of Foreign Exchange.* New York: St. Martin's Press.

Emery, Henry Crosby. 1896. *Speculation on the Stock and Produce Exchange of the United States.* New York: Columbia University Press.

"ETRADE—Yacht Life." 2017. YouTube. August 17. https://www.youtube.com/watch?v =Ux0-QwoOSBc.

"Fair Lending—Fair Lending Laws and Regulations." 2015. *FDIC Consumer Compliance Examination Manual.* September. https://www.fdic.gov/regulations/compliance /manual/4/iv-1.1.pdf.

Fama, Eugene. 1970. "Efficient Capital Markets: A Review of Theory and Empirical Work." *Journal of Finance* 25, no. 2: 383–417.

"Fidelity Investments TV Commercial, 'Clear and Straightforward Retirement Tools.'" 2017. iSpot.tv. https://www.ispot.tv/ad/wlxX/fidelity-investments-clear-and -straightforward-retirement-tools.

Foster, John Bellamy, and Fred Magdoff. 2009. *The Great Financial Crisis: Causes and Consequences.* New York: Monthly Review Press.

Fox, Justin. 2009. *The Myth of the Rational Market: A History of Risk, Reward, and Delusion on Wall Street.* New York: Harper Business.

Friedman, Milton. 1962. "The Methodology of Positive Economics." In *Essays in Positive Economics,* 3–43. Chicago: University of Chicago Press.

Frotman, Seth. 2018. "Broken Promises: How Debt-Financed Higher Education Rewrote America's Social Contract and Fueled a Quiet Crisis." *Utah Law Review* 4:811–46. https://dc.law.utah.edu/cgi/viewcontent.cgi?article=1172&context=ulr.

G, Anna. 2018. "Shocking Facts about Average Credit Card Debt." CreditDonkey.com. December 18. https://www.creditdonkey.com/average-credit-card-debt.html.

"The Giant Pool of Money." 2008. *This American Life.* WBEZ Chicago, Chicago Public Media. Produced by Ira Glass. May 9. Radio broadcast. https://www.thisamericanlife.org /355/the-giant-pool-of-money.

Gibson-Graham, J. K. 1996. *The End of Capitalism (as We Knew It): A Feminist Critique of Political Economy.* Minneapolis: University of Minnesota Press.

"Global CDO Issuance and Outstanding." 2015. Securities Industry and Financial Markets Association. January 13. Accessed July 19, 2016. http://www.sifma.org/uploadedFiles /Research/Statistics/StatisticsFiles/SF-Global-CDO-SIFMA.xls?n=19611.

Goodman, Laurie S. 2002. "Synthetic CDOS: An Introduction." *Journal of Derivatives* 9, no. 3: 60–72.

Gosselin, Peter. 2008. *High Wire: The Precarious Financial Lives of American Families*. New York: Basic Books.

Gramlich, Edward M. 2007. *Subprime Mortgages: America's Latest Boom and Bust*. Washington, DC: Urban Institute Press.

Grawert, Ames, and Tim Lau. 2019. "How the FIRST STEP Act Became Law—and What Happens Next." Brennan Center for Justice. January 4. https://www.brennancenter .org/blog/how-first-step-act-became-law-and-what-happens-next.

Green, Richard K., and Susan M. Wachter. 2005. "The American Mortgage in Historical and International Context." *Journal of Economic Perspectives* 19, no. 4: 93–114.

Greenspan, Alan. 1996. "The Challenge of Central Banking in a Democratic Society." Remarks at the Annual Dinner and Francis Boyer Lecture of the American Enterprise Institute for Public Policy Research, Washington, DC, December 5. https://www .federalreserve.gov/boarddocs/speeches/1996/19961205.htm.

Gromb, Denis, and Dimitri Vayanos. 2010. "Limits of Arbitrage: The State of the Theory." NBER Working Paper no. 15821.

Grossberg, Lawrence. 1992. *We Gotta Get out of This Place: Popular Conservatism and Postmodern Culture*. New York: Routledge.

Grossberg, Lawrence. 2017. "Wrestling with the Angels of Cultural Studies." In *Stuart Hall: Conversations, Projects and Legacies*, edited by David Morley and Julian Henriques, 107–16. London: Goldsmiths Press.

Grossberg, Lawrence, Carolyn Hardin, and Michael Palm. 2014. "Contributions to a Conjunctural Theory of Valuation." *Rethinking Marxism* 26, no. 3: 306–35.

Hacker, Jacob S. 2006. *The Great Risk Shift: The Assault on American Jobs, Families, Health Care, and Retirement and How You Can Fight Back*. New York: Oxford University Press.

Hardie, Ian. 2004. "'The Sociology of Arbitrage': A Comment on MacKenzie." *Economy and Society* 33, no. 2: 244–50.

Hardin, Carolyn. 2014. "Neoliberal Temporality: Time-Sense and the Shift from Pensions to 401(k)s." *American Quarterly* 66, no. 1: 95–118.

Hardin, Carolyn. 2017. "The Politics of Finance: Cultural Economy, Cultural Studies and the Road Ahead." *Journal of Cultural Economy* 10, no. 4: 325–38.

Hardin, Carolyn, and Adam Rottinghaus. 2015. "Introducing a Cultural Approach to Technology in Financial Markets." *Journal of Cultural Economy* 8, no. 5: 547–63.

Hardin, Carolyn, and Adam Rottinghaus. 2020. "Risk and Arbitrage." In *Routledge Handbook for Critical Finance Studies*, edited by Robert Wosnitzer and Christian Borch, 115–34. New York: Routledge.

Harvey, David. 1982. *The Limits to Capital*. Chicago: University of Chicago Press.

Harvey, David. 2005. *A Brief History of Neoliberalism*. New York: Oxford University Press.

Hayek, Friedrich A. von. 1945. "The Use of Knowledge in Society." *American Economic Review* 35, no. 4: 519–30.

Hayek, Friedrich A. von. [1944] 2007. *The Road to Serfdom*. Chicago: University of Chicago Press.

Holmes, Debbie. 2019. "Changes in Ohio Short-Term Lending Law Create New Loan Landscape." Cincinnati Public Radio. October 21. https://www.wvxu.org/post/changes-ohio-short-term-lending-law-create-new-loan-landscape.

"Home Ownership and President Bush." 2011. YouTube Video 6, no. 50. October 29. https://www.youtube.com/watch?v=bEmf78oPGCA.

Houge, Todd, and Jay Wellman. 2005. "Fallout from the Mutual Fund Trading Scandal." *Journal of Business Ethics* 62, no. 2: 129–39.

Hull, John C. 2008. *Fundamentals of Futures and Options Markets*. 6th ed. Upper Saddle River, NJ: Prentice Hall.

Hull, John C. 2009. *Options, Futures, and Other Derivatives*. 7th ed. Pearson International Edition. Upper Saddle River, NJ: Prentice Hall.

Hyman, Louis. 2011. *Debtor Nation: The History of America in Red Ink*. Princeton, NJ: Princeton University Press.

Ickes, Harold. 1953. *The Secret Diary of Harold Ickes*. New York: Simon and Schuster.

Ingham, Geoffrey. 2004. *The Nature of Money*. Malden, MA: Polity Press.

Inside Job. 2011. Directed by Charles Ferguson. New York: Sony Pictures Classics. DVD.

Investment Company Institute. 2018. "Retirement Assets Total $29.2 Trillion in Third Quarter." December 20.

Isard, Peter. 1977. "How Far Can We Push the 'Law of One Price'?" *American Economic Review* 67, no. 5: 942–48.

Jarrow, Robert A. 2012. "The Role of ABS, CDS, and CDOs in the Credit Crisis and the Economy." Paper presented at Rethinking Finance: Perspectives on the Crisis. New York. April 13.

Joseph, Miranda. 2014. *Debt to Society: Accounting for Life under Capitalism*. Minneapolis: University of Minnesota Press.

Kear, Mark. 2013. "Governing Homo Subprimicus: Beyond Financial Citizenship, Exclusion, and Rights." *Antipode* 45, no. 4: 926–46.

Kerr, Janet E., and John C. Maguire. 1988. "Program Trading—A Critical Analysis." *Washington and Lee Law Review* 45, no. 3: 991–1030.

Keynes, John Maynard. 1921. *A Treatise on Probability*. London: Macmillan.

Keynes, John Maynard. 1936. *The General Theory of Employment, Interest and Money*. London: Macmillan.

Kirzner, Israel M. 2008. "The Alert and Creative Entrepreneur: A Clarification." IFN Working Paper No. 760. Research Institute of Industrial Economics (IFN). Stockholm. http://hdl.handle.net/10419/81491.

Kiyosaki, Robert T., and Sharon L. Lechter. 1998. *Rich Dad, Poor Dad: What the Rich Teach Their Kids about Money That the Poor and Middle Class Do Not!* Paradise Valley, AZ: TechPress.

Knight, Frank H. [1921] 2014. *Risk, Uncertainty and Profit*. Eastford, CT: Martino Fine Books.

Kothari, Vinod. 2006. *Securitization: The Financial Instrument of the Future*. Hoboken, NJ: John Wiley and Sons.

Kwak, James. 2017. *Economism: Bad Economics and the Rise of Inequality*. New York: Pantheon Books.

Langley, Paul. 2008. *The Everyday Life of Global Finance: Saving and Borrowing in Anglo-America*. New York: Oxford University Press.

Lapavitsas, Costas. 2009. "Financialised Capitalism: Crisis and Financial Expropriation." *Historical Materialism* 17, no. 2: 114–48.

Latané, Henry A., and Richard J. Rendleman Jr. 1976. "Standard Deviations of Stock Price Ratios Implied in Option Prices." *Journal of Finance* 3, no. 2: 369–81.

Lauer, Josh. 2017. *Creditworthy: A History of Consumer Surveillance and Financial Identity in America*. New York: Columbia University Press.

Lee, Benjamin. 2016. "From Primitives to Derivatives." In *Derivatives and the Wealth of Societies*, edited by Lee and Martin, 2016, 82–139.

Lee, Benjamin, and Randy Martin. 2016. *Derivatives and the Wealth of Societies*. Chicago: University of Chicago Press.

Levitin, Michael. 2015. "The Triumph of Occupy Wall Street." *Atlantic*, June 10, 2015. https://www.theatlantic.com/politics/archive/2015/06/the-triumph-of-occupy-wall-street/395408/.

Lewis, Michael. 2014. *Flash Boys: A Wall Street Revolt*. New York: W. W. Norton.

LiPuma, Edward, and Benjamin Lee. 2004. *Financial Derivatives and the Globalization of Risk*. Durham, NC: Duke University Press.

MacKenzie, Donald. 2003. "Long-Term Capital Management and the Sociology of Arbitrage." *Economy and Society* 32, no. 3: 349–80.

MacKenzie, Donald. 2006. *An Engine, Not a Camera: How Financial Models Shape Markets*. Cambridge, MA: MIT Press.

MacKenzie, Donald. 2011. "The Credit Crisis as a Problem in the Sociology of Knowledge." *American Journal of Sociology* 116, no. 6: 1778–841.

MacKenzie, Donald. 2012. "Knowledge Production in Financial Markets: Credit Default Swaps, the ABX and the Subprime Crisis." *Economy and Society* 41, no. 3: 335–59.

MacKenzie, Donald, Daniel Beunza, Yuval Millo, and Juan Pablo Pado-Guerra. 2012. "Drilling through the Allegheny Mountains." *Journal of Cultural Economy* 5, no. 3: 279–96.

Madden, Mary, Michelle Gilman, Karen Levy, and Alice Marwick. 2017. "Privacy, Poverty and Big Data: A Matrix of Vulnerabilities for Poor Americans." *Washington University Law Review* 95: 53–125.

Mandel, Ernest. 1990. "Communism." In *Marxian Economics*, edited by John Eatwell, Murray Milgate, and Peter Newman, 87–90. New York: W. W. Norton.

Mann, Geoff. 2010a. "Hobbes' Redoubt? Toward a Geography of Monetary Policy." *Progress in Human Geography* 34, no. 5: 601–25.

Mann, Geoff. 2010b. "Value after Lehman." *Historical Materialism* 18, no. 4: 172–88.

Manning, Robert D. 2000. *Credit Card Nation: The Consequences of America's Addiction to Credit*. New York: Basic Books.

Marazzi, Christian. 2011. *The Violence of Financial Capitalism*. Translated by Kristena Lebedeva and Jason Francis McGimsey. Los Angeles: Semiotext(e).

Marron, Donncha. 2007. "'Lending by Numbers': Credit Scoring and the Constitution of Risk within American Consumer Credit." *Economy and Society* 36, no. 1: 103–33.

Marx, Karl. 1973. *Grundrisse: Foundations of the Critique of Political Economy (Rough Draft)*. Translated by Martin Nicolaus. New York: Penguin Books.

Marx, Karl. [1867] 2003. *Capital*. Vol. 1, *A Critical Analysis of Capitalist Production*. Edited by Friedrich Engels. New York: International Publishers.

Marx, Karl. [1894] 1991. *Capital*. Vol. 3, *The Process of Capitalist Production as a Whole*. Edited by Friedrich Engels. New York: Penguin Classics.

McCabe, Patrick. 2009. "The Economics of the Mutual Fund Trading Scandal." Federal Reserve Board, Finance and Economics Discussion Series Working Paper No. 2009–06, 14.

Meister, Robert. 2016. "Liquidity." In *Derivatives and the Wealth of Societies*, edited by Lee and Martin, 143–73.

Melamed, Jodi. 2006. "The Spirit of Neoliberalism: From Racial Liberalism to Neoliberal Multiculturalism." *Social Text* 24, no. 4: 1–24.

Melamed, Jodi. 2011. *Represent and Destroy: Rationalizing Violence in the New Racial Capitalism*. Minneapolis: University of Minnesota Press.

Merton, Robert. 1973. "Theory of Rational Option Pricing." *Bell Journal of Economics and Management Science* 4, no. 1: 141–83.

Michie, Ranald C. 1987. *The London and New York Stock Exchanges, 1850–1914*. London: Allen and Unwin.

Militello, Frederick C., Jr. 1984. "Growth of Arbitrage Changing Financial Management Practice." *AMA Forum* 73, no. 9.

Millstein, Ira. 1972. "Hearing on Availability of Credit to Women." Unpublished. Folder "Hearings and Related Records Availability of Credit to Women," box 35. RG Records of the National Commission of Consumer Finance, 1970–72, NARA, 3. May 22.

Mirowski, Philip. 2009. "Postface: Defining Neoliberalism." In Mirowski and Plehwe, *The Road from Mont Pelerin*, 417–54.

Mirowski, Philip, and Dieter Plehwe, eds. 2009. *The Road from Mont Pelerin: The Making of the Neoliberal Thought Collective*. Cambridge, MA: Harvard University Press.

Mirowski, Philip. 2009. "Postface: Defining Neoliberalism." In The Road from Mont Pelerin, edited by Philip Mirowksi and Dieter Plehwe, 417–54. Cambridge, MA: Harvard University Press.

Mishel, Lawrence, and Natalie Sabadish. 2012. "CEO Pay and the Top 1%: How Executive Compensation and Financial-Sector Pay Have Fueled Income Inequality." *Economic Policy Institute Report: Inequality and Poverty*. May 2. http://www.epi.org/publication/ib331-ceo-pay-top-1-percent/.

Miyazaki, Hirokazu. 2007. "Between Arbitrage and Speculation: An Economy of Belief and Doubt." *Economy and Society* 36, no. 3: 396–415.

Miyazaki, Hirokazu. 2013. *Arbitraging Japan: Dreams of Capitalism at the End of Finance*. Berkeley: University of California Press.

Modigliani, Franco, and Merton H. Miller. 1958. "The Cost of Capital, Corporation Finance and the Theory of Investment." *American Economic Review* 48, no. 3: 261–97.

Nichols, Robert. 2018. "Theft Is Property! The Recursive Logic of Dispossession." *Political Theory* 46, no. 1: 3–28.

Nocera, Joseph. 1994. *A Piece of the Action: How the Middle Class Joined the Money Class.* New York: Simon and Schuster.

"Northwestern Mutual TV Commercial, 'Spend Your Life Living: Ocean' Song by Cobra Starship." 2017. iSpot.tv. http://www.ispot.tv/ad/It3W/northwestern-mutual-spend -your-life-living-ocean.

"Occupy Wall Street: We are the 99%." OccupyWallStreet.org. Accessed February 27, 2019. http://occupywallst.org/.

O'Hara, Maureen. 2016. *Something for Nothing: Arbitrage and Ethics on Wall Street.* New York: W. W. Norton.

O'Shea, Arielle. 2019. "The Average 401(k) Balance by Age." NerdWallet. January 24. http://www.nerdwallet.com/article/the-average-401k-balance-by-age.

"Open-End Fund." 2018. Investopedia.com. Reviewed by James Chen. February 26. http://www.investopedia.com/terms/o/open-endfund.asp.

Ott, Julia. 2015. "Slaves: The Capital that Made Capitalism, a Re-Post." Public Seminar. August 20. http://www.publicseminar.org/2015/08/slaves-the-capital-that-made -capitalism/.

Parisi, Francis. 2004. "Loss Correlations among U.S. Consumer Assets." *Standard & Poor's,* New York. February.

Peters, John Durham. 2006. "Technology and Ideology: The Case of the Telegraph Revisited." In *Thinking with James Carey: Essays on Communications, Transportation, History,* edited by Jeremy Packer and Craig Robertson, 137–56. New York: Peter Lang.

Piwowar, Michael S. 2017. "SEC-NYU Dialogue on Exchange-Traded Products." Securities and Exchange Commission. September 8, 2017. https://www.sec.gov/news/speech /speech-piwowar-2017-09-08.

Plehwe, Dieter. 2009. Introduction to Mirowski and Plehwe, *The Road from Mont Pelerin,* 1–43.

Poitras, Geoffrey. 2010. "Arbitrage: Historical Perspectives." In *Encyclopedia of Quantitative Finance,* edited by Rama Cont, 1:1–10. Hoboken, NJ: John Wiley and Sons.

Pomroy, Kathryn. 2020. "Average Stock Market Return: Where Does 7% Come From?" *The Simple Dollar.* June 30. https://www.thesimpledollar.com/where-does-7-come -from-when-it-comes-to-long-term-stock-returns/.

Postone, Moishe. 1993. *Time, Labor, and Social Domination: A Reinterpretation of Marx's Critical Theory.* New York: Cambridge University Press.

"Predatory Lending Practices." 2001. C-SPAN. July 26. https://www.c-span.org/video/ ?165352-1/predatory-lending-practices.

Preston, John. 2010. "Concrete and Abstract Racial Domination." *Power and Education* 2, no. 2: 115–25.

"Prudential TV Commercial, 'The Prudential Walkways Experiment.'" 2017. iSpot. tv. https://www.ispot.tv/ad/wBUg/prudential-the-prudential-walkways -experiment.

Pulido, Laura. 2016. "Flint, Environmental Racism, and Racial Capitalism." *Capitalism Nature Socialism* 27, no. 3: 1–16.

Pulido, Laura. 2017. "Geographies of Race and Ethnicity II: Environmental Racism, Racial Capitalism and State-sanctioned Violence." *Progress in Human Geography* 41, no. 4: 524–33.

Ranganathan, Malini. 2016. "Thinking with Flint: Racial Liberalism and the Roots of an American Water Tragedy." *Capitalism Nature Socialism* 27, no. 3: 17–33.

Ranganathan, Malini. 2019. "Empire's Infrastructures: Racial Finance Capitalism and Liberal Necropolitics." *Urban Geography* 41, no. 4: 492–96.

Richardson, Matthew, and Lawrence J. White. 2009. "The Ratings Agencies: Is Regulation the Answer?" In Acharya and Richardson, *Restoring Financial Stability*, 101–15.

Rivlin, Gary. 2010. *Broke, USA: From Pawnshops to Poverty, Inc.—How the Working Poor Became Big Business.* New York: Harper and Row.

Robinson, Cedric J. 2000. *Black Marxism: The Making of the Black Radical Tradition.* 2nd ed. Chapel Hill: University of North Carolina Press.

Rosov, Sviatoslav. 2019. "SpaceX Is Opening Up the Next Frontier for HFT." *Market Integrity Insights.* June 25. https://blogs.cfainstitute.org/marketintegrity/2019/06/25/fspacex-is-opening-up-the-next-frontier-for-hft/.

Rothstein, Richard. 2014. "The Making of Ferguson: Public Policies at the Root of its Troubles." Economic Policy Institute Report, October 15. Accessed June 20, 2016. http://www.epi.org/publication/making-ferguson/.

Roye, Paul. 2001. "Speech by SEC Staff: Navigating the Mutual Fund Industry through Challenging Times." Securities and Exchange Commission. May 18. https://www.sec.gov/news/speech/spch491.htm.

Rubenstein, Mark. 2006. *A History of the Theory of Investments: My Annotated Bibliography.* Hoboken, NJ: John Wiley and Sons.

Rugh, Jacob S., Len Albright, and Douglas S. Massey. 2015. "Race, Space, and Cumulative Disadvantage: A Case Study of the Subprime Lending Collapse." *Social Problems* 62, no. 2: 186–218.

Russell-Kraft, Stephanie. 2013. "The Quantification of Finance: The Rise and Education of MFEs on Wall Street." Master's thesis, Humboldt University of Berlin.

"S&P 500." Yahoo! Finance. http://finance.yahoo.com/echarts?s=^gspc+interactive.

Santoni, G. J. 1988. "The October Crash: Some Evidence on the Cascade Theory." Federal Reserve Bank of St. Louis *Review*, May–June, 18–33. https://doi.org/10.20955/r.70.18-33.zcd.

Schor, Juliet B. 1998. *The Overspent American.* New York: Basic Books.

Schuhrke, Jeff. 2019. "We've Been Fighting for $15 for 7 Years. Today I'm Celebrating a Historic Victory." *Salon*, February 23. https://www.salon.com/2019/02/23/weve-been-fighting-for-15-for-7-years-today-im-celebrating-a-historic-victory_partner/.

Scott, Tim. 2017. "Senators Scott, Warner Champion Homeownership for the 'Credit Invisible.'" August 1. https://www.scott.senate.gov/media-center/press-releases/senators-scott-warner-champion-homeownership-for-the-credit-invisible.

Securities and Exchange Commission. 2013. "Net Asset Value." July 9. http://www.sec.gov/fast-answers/answersnavhtm.html.

Servon, Lisa. 2017. *The Unbanking of America: How the New Middle Class Survives.* Boston: Houghton Mifflin Harcourt.

Sharma, Sarah. 2014. *In the Meantime: Temporality and Cultural Politics.* Durham, NC: Duke University Press.

Shleifer, Andrei, and Robert W. Vishny. 1997. "The Limits of Arbitrage." *Journal of Finance* 52, no. 1: 35–55.

Sommeiller, Estelle, and Mark Price. 2018. "The New Gilded Age." Economic Policy Institute. July 19. http://www.epi.org/publication/the-new-gilded-age-income -inequality-in-the-u-s-by-state-metropolitan-area-and-county/.

Standing, Guy. 2011. *The Precariat: The Dangerous New Class.* New York: Bloomsbury.

"Strike Debt!" Accessed February 27, 2019. http://strikedebt.org/.

"Struggle for Black and Latino Mortgage Applicants Suggests Modern-Day Redlining." 2018. PBS *NewsHour.* PBS.org. Web video. February 15. http://www.pbs.org/newshour/show /struggle-for-black-and-latino-mortgage-applicants-suggests-modern-day-redlining.

"Survey of Consumer Finances." 2016. Federal Reserve. https://www.federalreserve.gov /econres/scfindex.htm.

Sweet, Elizabeth, Arijit Nandi, Emma Adam, and Thomas McWade. 2013. "The High Price of Debt: Household Financial Debt and Its Impact on Mental and Physical Health." *Social Science and Medicine* 91, no. 1: 94–100.

Taibbi, Matt. 2010. "The Great American Bubble Machine." *Rolling Stone,* April 5, 2010. https://www.rollingstone.com/politics/politics-news/the-great-american-bubble -machine-195229/.

Taleb, Nassim Nicholas. 2007. *The Black Swan: The Impact of the Highly Improbable.* New York: Random House.

Taylor, Keeanga-Yamahtta. 2019. *Race for Profit: How Banks and the Real Estate Industry Undermined Black Homeownership.* Chapel Hill: University of North Carolina Press.

Taylor, Winnie F. 2018. "The ECOA and Disparate Impact Theory: A Historical Perspective." *Journal of Law and Policy* 26, no. 2: 575–635. https://brooklynworks.brooklaw .edu/jlp/vol26/iss2/3/.

Tett, Gillian. 2009. *Fool's Gold: How the Bold Dream of a Small Tribe at J. P. Morgan Was Corrupted by Wall Street Greed and Unleashed a Catastrophe.* New York: Free Press.

Thomas, Jason, and Robert Van Order. 2010. "Housing Policy, Subprime Markets and Fannie Mae and Freddie Mac: What We Know, What We Think We Know and What We Don't Know." Paper presented at the Past, Present, and Future of the Government Sponsored Enterprises (GSE's) Conference. Federal Reserve Bank of St. Louis. https://files.stlouisfed.org/files/htdocs/conferences/gse/Van_Order.pdf.

"Timeline: 1960–1979." 2010. Wayback Machine. Accessed October 30, 2020. https://web .archive.org/web/20050420050328/http://www.nyse.com/about/history/timeline _1960_1979_index.html.

"Timeline of CME Achievements." 2015. CMEGroup.com. http://www.cmegroup.com /company/history/timeline-of-achievements.html.

Towns, Armond, and Carolyn Hardin. 2018. "Banking against (Black) Capitalism: On 'The Color of Money.'" *Los Angeles Review of Books,* March 19. https://lareviewofbooks.org/article/banking-against-black-capitalism-on-the-color-of-money.

Tribe, Keith. 2009. "Liberalism and Neoliberalism in Britain, 1930–1980." In Mirowski and Plehwe, *The Road from Mont Pelerin,* 68–97.

United States, Financial Crisis Inquiry Commission. 2011. *The Financial Crisis Inquiry Report: Final Report of the National Commission on the Causes of the Financial and Economic Crisis in the United States.* Authorized edition. New York: Public Affairs.

"US Mortgage Related Issuance and Outstanding." 2020. SIFMA. October 6, 2020. Accessed October 30, 2020. https://www.sifma.org/resources/research/us-mbs-issuance-and-outstanding/.

"Value at Risk (VaR)." 2019. Investopedia. Reviewed by Will Kenton. February 17. https://www.investopedia.com/terms/v/var.asp.

Van Horn, Rob, and Philip Mirowski. 2009. "The Rise of the Chicago School of Economics and the Birth of Neoliberalism." In Mirowski and Plehwe, *The Road from Mont Pelerin,* 139–79.

Vercellone, Carlo. 2010. "The Crisis of the Law of Value and the Becoming-Rent of Profit." In *Crisis in the Global Economy: Financial Markets, Social Struggles, and New Political Scenarios,* edited by Andrea Fumagalli and Sandro Mezzadra, translated by Jason Francis McGimsey, 85–118. Los Angeles: Semiotext(e).

von Neumann, John, and Oskar Morgenstern. 1944. *Theory of Games and Economic Behavior.* Princeton, NJ: Princeton University Press.

Weinstein, Meyer H. 1931. *Arbitrage in Securities.* New York: Harper and Brothers.

White, Micah. 2015. "Protest Is Broken." Blog post. Accessed February 18, 2018. https://www.micahmwhite.com/protest-is-broken.

Williams, Brett. 2004. *Debt for Sale: A Social History of the Credit Trap.* Philadelphia: University of Pennsylvania Press.

Williams, Raymond. 1977. *Marxism and Literature.* Oxford: Oxford University Press.

Williams, Sean. 2016. "Here's How Much the Average American Has in an IRA, Sorted by Age." *Fox Business,* June 27. https://www.foxbusiness.com/markets/heres-how-much-the-average-american-has-in-an-ira-sorted-by-age.amp.

Wolfe, Tom. 1988. *The Bonfire of the Vanities.* New York: Farrar, Straus and Giroux.

Wolff, Richard D., and Stephen A. Resnick. 1987. *Economics: Marxian versus Neoclassical.* Baltimore: Johns Hopkins University Press.

Wosnitzer, Robert. 2014. "Desk, Firm, God, Country: Proprietary Trading and Speculative Ethos of Financialism." PhD diss., Department of Media, Culture, and Communication, New York University.

Wyly, Elvin, C. S. Ponder, Pierson Nettling, Bosco Ho, Sophie Ellen Fung, Zachary Liebowitz, and Dan Hammel. 2012. "New Racial Meanings of Housing in America." *American Quarterly* 64, no. 3: 571–604.

Zaloom, Caitlin. 2006. *Out of the Pits: Traders and Technology from Chicago to London.* Chicago: University of Chicago Press.

Zitzewitz, Eric. 2003. "Who Cares About Shareholders? Arbitrage-Proofing Mutual Funds." *Journal of Law, Economics, and Organization* 19, no. 2: 245–80.

Page numbers followed by f refer to figures

Wall Street, 7, 28, 29–30, 63, 94, 105. *See also* Dodd-Frank Wall Street Reform and Consumer Protection Act; Occupy Wall Street (ows)
Warner, Mark, 127
Weinstein, Meyer, 58
welfare (social), 31, 83, 125, 128
welfare state, 25, 77. *See also* asset-based welfare
Wellman, Jay, 69–70

Wells Fargo, 118
White, Lawrence, 109
William, John Burr, 134n3
Wolff, Richard, 13, 72, 131n1
World War I, 60
World War II, 21, 94
Wosnitzer, Robert, 77
Wyly, Elvin, 118

Zitzewitz, Eric, 71